Working with Real People

The Challenging and the Inspirational

Brian M. Breacher

authorHOUSE®

AuthorHouse™ UK Ltd.
500 Avebury Boulevard
Central Milton Keynes, MK9 2BE
www.authorhouse.co.uk
Phone: 08001974150

First published by AuthorHouse 10/17/2008

ISBN: 978-1-4389-1776-4 (sc)
ISBN: 978-1-4389-1777-1 (hc)

Printed in the United States of America
Bloomington, Indiana

This book is printed on acid-free paper.

Contents

Chapter 1: Introduction 1
Chapter 2: Relationships Are Very Important 3
Chapter 3: The Village 8
Chapter 4: Fatal Road Traffic Accidents 31
Chapter 5: Time For a Change 36
Chapter 6: Working With Young People 38
Chapter 7: The Next Phase of My Adventures
                    – and More Challenges...45
Chapter 8: Thinking Ahead 51
Chapter 9: History, Human Nature and Spirituality...............71
Chapter 10: It Had to Be Experienced to Be Believed 75
Chapter 11: People Struggling to Deal With Pressure and Stress.....81
Chapter 12: Dealing With Extremes 84
Chapter 13: The Attendance Centre...88
Chapter 14: The Young People's Befriending Scheme 92
Chapter 15: Afterwards – Filling the Gap................................102

Chapter 1: Introduction

Through being a police officer from 1960 – 1990, then running a registered charity afterwards for a further fourteen years, I am extremely fortunate in being able to look back upon a rare collection of privileged insights into other people's lives that was my experience on a daily basis throughout my whole working life.

Dealing with folk in the real world at such close quarters is an unusual opportunity that few people have the chance to visualise in such a way. This may well be why I am still trying to make sense of the challenges, the adventures and the constant learning opportunities in which I was involved over a total period of forty four years!

People rarely ever assume that a reported crime is likely to be detected or that justice will prevail; nor does it often cross the mind of a criminal that his misbehaviour will be uncovered. In reality, the thrill of successfully detecting and prosecuting a crime can provide the motivation that urges you to work every day.

There is almost always a way of solving a crime, given sufficient time, and the means involved in doing so can be intense, combative, confrontational, and extremely satisfying.

Whilst struggling to suppress the dark side of their nature, the antagonists are often arrogant and self-righteous; and in any event behaviour with self-preservation in mind knows few bounds.

Those who understand that they need your help are usually co-operative and supportive; and the experience can be truly amazing when you connect with decent right-thinking people. The sharing of a worthy responsibility with them is, in large part, what keeps you inspired and energised.

One of the most enlightened quotes I have read in recent times said, "Rules are made for the guidance of wise men and the obedience of fools." One message that can be taken from this is that responsible positions of authority should be handled above all with maturity, flexibility and common sense.

For the last eighteen years since my retirement, I have tried to make sense of these challenges. But I have come to the conclusion that the rights and wrongs of how I managed my role as a public servant are for others to make up their mind. Did I do a reasonable job or not – you decide?

Brian Breacher

In the interests of confidentiality and to prevent embarrassing anyone, I have avoided the mention of true names and places.

Chapter 2: Relationships Are Very Important

When I knew that I was coming to England to join the police service at twenty two years of age, I decided I would take my own way of life with me and endeavour to meet a range of ordinary, decent folk and work towards interacting with them.

I also thought that, as I would essentially be working for the public, it would be important to seek approval and support for the way I functioned as a police officer, from the people I met outside the service. The imperative would be to strike a reasonable balance somewhere between the way they approved of how I operated and the methods adopted by my colleagues.

I wanted to ensure that my own values and ideals would be aligned with people I respected, which included those with whom I had grown up who always remained important to me.

Initially I was a little uncomfortable in the police service and thought I would just have to be patient and see how my experiences would develop. Thankfully, I grew to enjoy the challenges a great deal, and supporting or networking with all manner of people was a very privileged position to be in; though I still occasionally felt ill at ease on the police inner circle.

Nevertheless, it was reassuring to know that to a large extent you could adopt your own personal style, even in the police force, if you worked hard enough to discover how this could be managed.

You may sometimes feel on your own when your environment does not always seem to make sense. But as soon as you learn how to absorb the pressure and manoeuvre around the obstacles, you discover that this state of affairs serves to heighten the satisfaction of overcoming all the odds. Though you really do need a clear idea of where you stand, along with the support and trust of people you respect.

My first risqué experience of living in England

My first living accommodation was in a council house that was found for me by my new employer. As soon as I was taken there to meet the landlady and her husband I was certain that I was about to encounter my very first challenge, for I would never of my own choosing have considered this a suitable place to live. The lady and her husband lacked any kind of sparkle and also lodging in the same house was a young woman of similar disposition to the landlady.

After residing there for about two weeks, I was getting ready for bed one night when suddenly I heard a sound from just behind my bedroom door. I turned around to catch a glimpse of my landlady and her other lodger, peering through the fanlight window above my door. As they quickly dodged out of sight they seemed to stumble off the chair on which they must both have been struggling to keep balanced!

This really wasn't the kind of friendship I had in mind when I came to England, for it was altogether a very odd experience. I thought it best to say nothing to these two women for I had not planned to stay there any longer than I could avoid. I came to realise that the other lodger was a likeable character in many ways, with a sense of humour but very sad at times.

Two days later I managed to escape after a neighbour living a few doors away, who by chance happened to come from my own part of the world, spoke to me as I was passing-by.

He said, "Whoever put you in there must have been bloody mad. You can come and stay with us for a while, until you find a more suitable place." He was an interesting and respectable character who was a scientist at a local research and development establishment, a keen player of golf and a former speedway rider. I was very happy for quite a few months living with this generous person and his wife who happened to be a great cook.

So much violence

Of course I had already seen plenty of drunken people but when it became my duty to confront them so often I was surprised by how violent they could be; and they always seemed to want to fight each other.

I had not joined the police service to become a punch bag for anyone, so from an early stage of my career I decided to join a sports club or two. This allowed me to train with some lively and competitive people and maintain a reasonable level of fitness. I respected them and enjoyed their company and they were very supportive when I was on duty. The men who ran the club were really decent, highly thought of individuals.

It proved to be extremely useful to meet so many fit and tough people and to have them on my side. Several times when they saw me on duty outside local dance halls they would say, "Hi Brian, if you have any trouble mate, give us a shout." Luckily, I never did have any trouble but I regarded the fact that I had friends like this who were so sympathetic in this way, as quite novel in the general scheme of things.

I met my wife after just two weeks and I really could not believe how lucky I was. We socialized together with her circle of friends, her hockey club, horse riding and political club. We went dancing at a social club and met people in a variety of other situations too.

I later joined a local squash club, ran for the Force cross-country team and mixed with many people at church. I had previously been of a different Christian denomination to my wife, but it became far more convenient for us to attend her church together.

Confidence gained from wearing the uniform

My first arrest occurred right out of the blue. I was on foot patrol in the High Street of a large town on a busy shopping day, quietly trying to fit into the role of my new job as appropriately as I perceived that people would wish. The personal feelings I experienced throughout this process were quite special.

Suddenly, a couple of young lads ran up to me to say that two men were in the park just about one hundred and fifty yards away, and they were fighting with a knife. This public park was a really attractive place full of flowers and neat, fertile grass. It was used mainly by families, children and retired people alike.

I walked there at a brisk pace, whilst keeping my thoughts open and my demeanour in check and using the opportunity for a moment's thinking time.

As I arrived at the scene the men were still squaring up to each other, and one of them was brandishing a large, polished sheath knife that glistened menacingly as it reflected the sun. A number of people were anxiously watching them – from a safe distance. When I stepped between them, I was aware of an underlying impression that they both were glad I had arrived before the situation had grown more seriously out of hand, which was helpful from my own point of view.

One of the men had sustained a quite severe stab wound to his thigh which was still bleeding. The second man with the knife seemed to be a tough and sturdy individual, who I suspected was already beginning to feel some regret for what had happened.

I took the knife from him and instructed someone to call for an ambulance (there were no personal radios in those days). I took brief details from the injured man; then arrested the knife wielding assailant and walked with him a few hundred yards to the police station. I chatted with him to keep him relaxed, as I firmly held his wrist throughout his short march into custody.

During this incident, I was quite surprised by how accepting he was that I had taken control. He offered no resistance and it was particularly reassuring to discover that my presence in uniform had been so influential and effective.

It was significant that no animosity was shown between us, either way. It also helped a great deal that our emotions remained calm and we were both comfortable in showing each other a measure of respect.

The Vicar's cold-frame

I was young in service driving a police car and waiting at the traffic lights, when I heard a motor cycle overtake me and race through the lights which were still at red. The motor cycle rider turned sharp left into the market place just ahead but glanced off one of the metal stanchions that marked the perimeter of the square, and he was thrown forward from his machine.

He somehow managed to maintain his balance as he abandoned his bike to run off down the road. I thought to myself, 'Here we go again,' so I drove into the market place just in time to see him run into a cobbled lane about 100 yards down the hill. I left my vehicle, which I had no time to lock, and chased him along the footway.

I gained ground on him just in time to see him approach a shoulder high wall and clamber over it. As his feet landed on the other side, they crashed right through a glass cold-frame in what was the local vicar's garden. As this was happening, I leapt forward so that I was balanced with my stomach on top of the wall, and I managed to grab hold of him. I yanked him back over the wall and we tussled vigorously on the floor until I managed to subdue him.

Back at the police station he continued to swear and yell abuse. When I ignored his threats and began recording his personal details, he suddenly became physically aggressive again and threw a punch at me, which I avoided.

He then head-butted me and aimed for my face, but I managed to draw back and he just caught my eye, though only slightly. I struck him square on the jaw and he fell to the ground.

In Court, where he appeared for riding whilst under the influence of drugs, his solicitor asked me if I would agree that I had assaulted his client. "Yes," I said, "He aimed two blows at me but I only hit him once." The Court considered that this was most acceptable on my part; and so did I.

A humbling experience

When I was in my first year of service one ordinary day - or that's what people might assume, I was in uniform and on foot patrolling an extremely pleasant market town, which at that time I enjoyed for virtually eight hours of every day.

I happened to be standing at the edge of the busy market square, when suddenly I felt a little hand pushing into mine and which I clasped firmly. I looked down to see a picture of innocence – a little girl aged about seven years looking up at me, and who then asked if I would please take her across the road.

I glanced back to see her mother giving me a smile and a gentle nod of approval and off I went across the road with this little person. I don't know how she felt but I regarded this experience as a distinct privilege that left me glowing for quite a while afterwards.

A lady in distress

When I was patrolling the cobbled streets of the town on another occasion, a very smartly dressed lady aged about thirty years, who I had noticed in the street a few times before, came to me with a smile and a look of relief on her face.

She said that she had just had an accident with her skirt and asked if I could pin her zip together with the safety pin that she handed to me.

With some disbelief I knelt down at her side on one knee and duly fastened the zip of her skirt. I was amazed that this woman had entrusted me with such a delicate task!

Chapter 3: The Village

As soon as we were married, my wife and I moved to a delightful village in the south midlands where it was a real pleasure to work and live for eight years. We made a happy start to our married life there, making many friends, and our two sons were born there also. After a short time my wife and I became good friends with the local vicar and his wife.

The vicar ran confirmation classes that I attended and I was baptised in his church just before being formally confirmed. For several years I served on his church committee and with another decanal team covering a wider rural area.

The vicar gave me lots of encouragement and he always seemed fascinated by the interesting things I dealt with. I know that he often listened-in to the police vhf radio during evening time, for he would sometimes invite me around the next day for coffee, and to share some of the juicy details of events he knew I had attended.

I never disclosed any confidential information but I always did my best to satisfy his sense of innocent curiosity.

The people

The community in our village was very special and there were many exceptional people who were first class neighbours.

After my wife and I got to know a farming family quite well, we attended many church events and went on holiday together. I helped with the haymaking a few times, for the sheer pleasure of a new, physical and healthy experience.

I enjoyed the camaraderie here and the exercise and hard work out in the sun. I especially looked forward to the refreshment our friend the farmer's wife brought out into the fields for lunch. This was typically delicious, wholesome, nourishing country fare, produced right there on the farm. Mechanical assistance was far more limited in those days of course but haymaking was probably more fun, especially for the opportunity it gave to share and enjoy a great sense of community spirit.

The surrounding hills were rugged and full of character and the meadows on the lower slopes were particularly green and lush, productive and well manicured.

I really felt a part of the community when, for the sake of safety and in uniform, I brought up the rear of my farmer friend's cattle as he drove all his livestock along the main road when he upgraded his farming business and took over the new glebe farm at the edge of the village.

This particular farming family did so much for the village and they were always contributing if not leading one village activity or another. They held pig roasts, barn dances and jazz concerts; as well as helping to run the local fetes, which were always very well attended; they visited older people and were involved in many other enterprising community activities.

The farm manager of the local estate was from a small town in Scotland. He and I had a very good relationship from which we both profited – I had the freedom to run around the estate, whilst I made myself available to assist him most of the time.

When I first met this farmer he told me that the Scout Troup from my home town in Wales had beaten his team in a major scouting jamboree in 1926, before going on to win the Commonwealth Scouting Championship in that event.

In hot pursuit

It was an amazing coincidence that a school friend of mine from my home town in south Wales came to live in the same village and we were able to renew our old friendship. He lived with his wife and young family and taught at the local school.

He came to see me at my home one day, mystified because someone had stolen some personal items from their clothes line overnight. These included his best shirt that he was due to wear to the teachers' ball that evening, his wife's nightdress and a table-cloth they had received as a wedding gift.

I went to his home at the top of a three storey block of flats, so that my enquiries could begin logically where the theft had taken place; and I listened to the sketchy details of what had happened.

I asked whether he or his wife could recall seeing or hearing anything suspicious or unusual during late evening in the garden down below, where the clothes had been left to dry overnight. They said "No, nothing at all." I asked them to reflect on anything at all that might have happened but again they said that nothing in particular came to mind.

They may have been unaware of what I regarded as suspicious or significant, so I again asked them to really concentrate on any detail whatsoever they could remember from the previous evening. They then told me that because their dog was on heat their attention had been drawn to another dog they had not seen before, which was in the gardens down below.

They said it was like a sheep dog, black and white in colour and they thought it had been on its own.

I knew of a dog like the one they had seen, and wondered whether anyone who might have been with it could have noticed anything at all helpful. So I went immediately to the home of the dog's owner, a rather cheerful coach driver who lived with his wife just a couple of hundred yards or so from the flats.

I knocked on the door, and he immediately greeted me with a resigned, knowing smile and a noticeable sense of relief. "Come on in guv, I've probably got just what you're looking for, right here," he said.

I went into his living room and he opened a chest of drawers to take out all the 'stolen' clothes, in one neatly laundered pile, and he handed them carefully over to me.

"That wretched dog of ours," he said. "When we got up this morning we found these clothes strewn all across our rear lawn. We were just trying to work out who they could belong to!"

I thanked him for the way he had been so helpful and I praised his wife for laundering them so promptly; and I took them straightaway to the owners.

The timescale from taking the details from my teacher friend, right up to returning the missing clothes, all neatly washed and ironed – and free of unnecessary formalities, was no more than about fifteen minutes in total. Needless to say, the rightful owners were thrilled to get them back so promptly, especially in good condition and all ready to use!

The following Sunday, this story, complete with picture, was published in the News of the World, simply because a woman's nightdress had been involved. For my part, I failed to see anything at all salacious about a dog jumping up at a nightdress, which, for the purpose of the picture, the photographer encouraged it to do by hiding a ball in some garment!

Whiskey the dog was bright, energetic and lovable and completely unaware that he had just made national news. He became the only thief I can ever recall who was absolutely admired and loved by everyone in the neighbourhood!

The village telephone box

One of the women in the village was a mine of useful information and she was always interested in supporting the work I did. She once told me she was anxious about the obscene telephone calls she had begun to receive at her home.

I gave her the usual advice about keeping a detailed log of events, using a recording machine for the calls, or directing a very high pitched personal alarm into the telephone.

I also told her how difficult it was to trace and detect this kind of offender, as it was in those days, the mid-sixties. She said the offending male had a north-western accent and often she could even hear young children in the background.

During this same period, I sometimes visited the home of a lady who was a strong individual, with a tough job on a farm and who I greatly respected. She had two small children and an older son. She also had a husband she did not trust, mainly because of his unstable sexual habits.

From time to time, she would confide in me and share the details of what she thought he was getting up to, in case any innocent people were likely to be at risk.

Her husband, who was a motor mechanic by trade, also happened to have a north-western accent.

About a year or more afterwards I was in the village High Street late one evening, when by chance I noticed a man in the local telephone box.

For some reason, it occurred to me that it might be the farm worker's husband, so I made my way across the road to check in this unlit corner which was further darkened by overhanging trees.

It was the very man I had in mind, so I went closer to the box. The door was slightly ajar hanging on damaged hinges and I could clearly hear him using a boy's voice to enquire as to the colour of the underwear being worn by the person to whom he was speaking. He asked another question of a personal nature before reverting to his own voice.

He claimed that he was a G.P.O. engineer, who as a result of a spate of complaints, was trying to trace the telephone from where the 'boy' was calling.

He went on to say that if she could bear to listen to some more of the boy's conversation, there would be a very good chance of him being traced.

He then changed back again to the boy's voice and carried on with the same kind of highly personal and intrusive questions.

He made three telephone calls one after the other and all in the same vein, whilst I was deciding upon the time at which I could safely say that there was sufficient evidence for me to intervene.

I needed also to think about how I could identify the victims – and especially the woman he would be telephoning at the time I chose to become involved. I also had to consider how I would deal with this tricky individual, because in those days there was no easy system for tracing telephone calls.

I decided that I had to be satisfied with what I had heard so far, which was already quite substantial, or I would risk losing the chance to speak with any of the aggrieved women on the other end of the telephone.

At that point, I swung the door wide open, took the telephone out of his hands and blocked his escape with my body. I then spoke calmly into the telephone to identify myself to the person on the other end of the line. I asked the woman to telephone the main police station and to leave her name and address there, so that I could get in touch with her later.

I then interviewed the man and told him what I had overheard and quoted the offence that was involved. True to form, he denied that he had made any such call and feigned indignation about having such serious allegations made against him.

In those days, there was no power of arrest for that particular crime, so I told him that he would be hearing more about this matter in due course.

When I returned to the police station I found that, according to plan, the lady had left her details for me. I then contacted the police in the adjoining county where she lived and asked them to visit her to take a witness statement covering all aspects of identity, conversation, continuity and the emotional effect the call had upon her.

The police at once told me they had already received identical complaints that evening from several women in the same area, who had all been extremely distressed.

Statements were taken from all the women, which described a man with a matching accent and an overwhelmingly similar pattern of behaviour, or method of operation, which helped to prove they had all been victims of the same seedy individual. All of the women happened to live some twenty miles from the telephone box where the calls were made.

It appeared that he would telephone a random number and if he succeeded in speaking to a woman who was taken in by him, he would then use the same telephone prefix to speak to several more potential female victims; thus, many offences would occur in the same general location.

Because he pleaded 'not guilty', our Chief Prosecutor took the case, which he usually did if they were particularly interesting, and the five women were required to attend court to share the details of each squalid conversation, in open court. One of them was sick just as her time to enter the witness box approached and she had to be consoled.

Thankfully he was found guilty and was sentenced to a heavy fine.

At the end of the case, his defence solicitor said he had been fascinated by how his client had been caught and successfully brought to court. And the woman in my own village received no further obscene telephone calls.

I don't know how the offender's wife reacted but she was far stronger than him, so I feel certain that she would have coped.

Boys will be boys

I was walking through the village one mid-afternoon, when I saw two lads aged about ten years who I knew well. They were from an estate nearby and just at that moment were inside one of the two village telephone boxes.

I guessed they were very unlikely to be there for any justifiable purpose and, in true 'naughty boy' mode, I saw them in turn spitting on the small glass panels of the box to see whose spittle would dribble down the furthest!

I knew their families well, as both their older brothers were often in trouble with the law. The father of one lad was such a poor role model that he once wanted to continue watching a cowboy film on the television, rather than listen to what I had to say about his older son who had become involved in something quite serious. However, I was aware that the parents of both boys were rather more weak than they were bad.

After having a few words with them I sent the two boys home to fetch a bucket of hot water, and a duster and hand brush. They went away without any argument and returned within ten minutes suitably equipped, as I had expected.

I instructed them on how to give the telephone box a good cleaning and then to do the same with the one at the other end of the village.

The Post Mistress, whose office was directly opposite the second telephone box, later told me that when she saw them arrive and clean the phone box without any supervision, she just couldn't believe her eyes. She said they had beavered away inside and out, until they made the box look very respectable indeed.

I later thanked the boys for the spirit in which they had made amends for their original indiscretion and praised them for the standard of work they had managed to achieve.

A novel telephone call

The Post Mistress then took the opportunity to tell me that she wished I could do something about the noise and bad language that she and her neighbours had to put up with on several nights each week. A small group of men, she said, were in the habit of turning out drunk after midnight from one of the local public houses. I told her I would do my best to see what I could do about this problem.

Two nights later just after midnight, I heard the shouting and swearing that was becoming such a regular nuisance for people in the neighbourhood. I went to the top of the village and saw two men struggling to walk home - down the centre of the main road.

I approached the first of them who was swearing loudly in very boisterous mood. I asked him to keep the noise down but the other man joined him and he was even more rowdy and aggressive.

After telling the second person to tone down the noise he became very argumentative and increased the volume further. I asked for his name and address but he refused to say.

He said he wanted to complain about me, which was a means sometimes used for diverting attention. In any event it is virtually impossible to reason with someone so drunk. He followed me down to the centre of the village to the police office.

When we arrived there, I suggested he came back in the morning if he wanted to complain, for the office was empty because it was already past one o'clock in the morning.

He turned around and lurched off back towards the other end of the village. As he was doing so, I popped into the police office where a list of telephone numbers for all public telephone boxes in the area was kept.

I watched until he neared the one at the top end of the village, then I dialled the number.

Curiosity got the better of him of course and he picked up the telephone. I enquired, "Who is that?" He said, "It's George Williams." I then asked, "And where do you live then George?" "380 High Street, he replied." I thanked him and said I would see him next morning, which I did and cautioned him about his behaviour. The noise problem was duly sorted.

This man, I later discovered, worked hard on the local estate and when he was sober he was quite an affable and energetic individual with a sense of humour. We were both necessary members of the same thriving community and mutual co-operation and friendship from that point onwards was soon established.

The concerned lorry driver

As it was just becoming dark during another evening, I received a telephone call from a lorry driver using the same village call box.

He told me that his heavy goods vehicle had broken down near a bend just outside of the village and in the thickening fog. In a feigned tone of courtesy, he said that in the interests of safety he felt that someone ought to be informed.

After I thanked him he told me his name was Mr Smith. I then recognised his voice as I recalled meeting him about a year previously in a nearby police station just after a colleague had arrested him for burglary and assault.

"That's Mr Salter, isn't it?" I said. "Well it is actually," he replied. I thought it best to visit his lorry to make sure it was safe and because there might be something else amiss - which he had conveniently chosen not to mention! Sure enough I found stolen property on his vehicle which needed a lot of explaining.

My interview with him next day in a near-by town, in the street outside his home, proved to be quite an adventure. He and his two criminal associates tried very hard at close quarters to intimidate me and disrupt my enquiry. I had already made sure that my investigation was virtually complete but for the need to seize the final piece of evidence from his vehicle in his presence.

Immediately after conclusion, I just managed to avoid their attempt to surround me. Then as I sat astride my motor cycle before I rode away, each began jabbing a finger within a few inches of my chest; though by this time I had already managed to achieve all of my objectives!

As I drove away, I experienced a surge of adrenalin because of having just side-stepped the obstructive and threatening behaviour of these three tricky characters.

I did not regard them as a very real threat, either to myself or to the local community as a whole. Neither did I believe that what I had just achieved was in any way likely to bring an end to thoughts on their part of even more dubious activities.

They were probably incapable of putting together any serious criminal enterprise that called for a modicum of forethought or intelligence.

Taking a break

I met a gentle and really interesting retired couple who were living in a remote village. The lady's grandfather had been a Regimental Sergeant Major at the Battle of Balaclava in October 1854. Their cottage was full of historical memorabilia, including a photograph of the woman's grandfather, in the ceremonial uniform of his regiment, in sepia.

They were experiencing problems with a local farmer who they said had dumped cow silage across a bridleway near where they lived, and which they considered to be offensive.

The lady had a tendency to talk non-stop for long periods of time, which did not normally pose any difficulty for me. I realised that she was very keen to convince me that this problem required my urgent attention and there was so much she wanted to say. In any event she was a very sweet person.

Later on, she telephoned me during the course of this dispute, to update me on events in her neighbourhood. The problem on this occasion was that I simply had an urgent need to attend the loo! I did not want to stop her speaking whilst she was in full flow, even if I could, so I nipped to the loo and hurried back afterwards.

Luckily, as I had anticipated – and hoped, she had not realised I was missing for those few moments and the lady was still talking enthusiastically about the same subject when I returned. Thankfully, the problem was satisfactorily resolved in due course.

The young driver and his co-conspirator

I saw a young lad driving unaccompanied, through the village High Street in a white van and knew he had not yet passed his driving test, which among other things meant that he would not have any insurance for his vehicle. In the scheme of things this would be quite serious, for not only would he be a danger to other people, it was well known that he frequently set a bad example to his younger brothers.

The next day when I saw him, I said I would report him for those offences. But he replied that I would never prove them.

When he eventually appeared in Court, he asserted that at the time I claimed to have seen him, he was elsewhere with a friend, who gave evidence in support of this story. He was found 'not guilty', which bothered me a great deal.

I felt certain that the naivety of the combined forces that led to this result, would also guide him towards more serious trouble. I also knew that other lads, with whom he spent his time, might see this as an opportunity for them to adopt a similar frame of mind and follow him by taking more risks themselves.

I knew that he and his friend had conspired together and seriously perjured themselves, which was something I would deal with as a matter of urgency. So I decided to spend the next week or so finding a solution to this village problem.

It is tempting to assume that you must raise your sights to a different level when thinking through this sort of dilemma. But the fact is you must first consider whether an answer might be staring you right in the face.

In the course of investigating crime, you normally endeavour to avoid involving other people unnecessarily, but when blatant lies are told in Court on oath, you have to be prepared to muster support from people you would not normally want to inconvenience.

The following morning, I called to see Richard's next-door neighbour and asked if she remembered seeing him on that particular day when he had driven the van on his own.

"Oh yes," she said. "In fact I was only across the road from you when I believe you saw him too." She even remembered the day and date.

I then went to Richard's neighbour on the other side and asked her the same question. "Yes," she also replied, "I remember the date because it was the day of the postmen's strike and I was worried about getting a birthday card to my daughter. I saw Richard arrive in his van on his own, he went in doors and then drove off again shortly afterwards, again on his own."

I was a little surprised at their willingness to become involved but I suspect their maternal instincts and common sense made them feel anxious for the safety of all the young children in the neighbourhood. Richard and his co-conspirator were arrested the same day. When presented with the additional evidence, they owned up to crimes of both conspiracy and perjury. In his explanation, Richard said, "I knew Mr Breacher wouldn't let me get away with that!"

The pied piper

During the mid-sixties and about five years into my service, I was driving alone at midnight in a patrol car in the rural area where I worked. I was directed to an incident that was taking place in a remote village at the top of a hill. I had no idea what I was being sent to because the radio reception was so fragmented.

As I approached the village, the main street seemed awash with people and a few cars, and some anxious residents were even viewing the scene from their opened bedroom windows.

At first sight, it appeared as though I had arrived at a road accident.

After parking my car, I walked to the centre of a group of about eight youths and I attempted to find out exactly what the problem was.

At that point someone threw a large bottle which shattered into fragments about my feet.

This may well seem a potentially fraught state of affairs but when you are cold sober and have a specific purpose in mind, it is not at all such a hopeless situation. In an odd sort of way, it can sometimes be helpful when everyone around you is hyped up with a mixture of alcohol, ill will and Dutch courage.

The youths in the street were very surly and offered a series of unintelligent and downright obstructive responses to a few questions that I had asked simply to find out what was happening and whether anyone had been injured.

It was obvious that the focus of their aggression was mainly towards the occupants of a house close-by, so I decided that the starting point for my enquiries should be re-directed to the young people with whom they were locked in dispute.

I received an encouraging welcome into the house and sought to discover grounds for taking some form of positive action that would bring the problem to a close. The young men and women in the house told me they had been enjoying a private party but were prevented from going home because of threats and intimidation from the gang outside. I asked whether anything specific such as an assault, damage or theft, had actually happened out in the street and was told by a youth that his jacket had been badly damaged after being slashed with a sheath knife by one of the gang.

This then provided me with a power of arrest but the first lad was unwilling to come outside with me to identify the culprit with the knife.

I asked whether anyone else had witnessed this happening and a second youth came forward to say that he had also seen the incident. I enquired if they would both come outside with me to point out the offender, and with some reluctance the two of them eventually agreed.

Out in the street, they freely indicated a lad who was now sitting in a car with his father who had just arrived to take him home. I asked them within his hearing, whether he was the one who had used the knife and they assured me that he was.

I asked them again if they were certain and they both said "Yes". Because evidence of identification is so important and mistakes can very easily be made, I turned again to ask them a third time, but they had become unnerved and were already retreating once more to the safety of the house.

I nevertheless asked the lad to leave the car so that I could search him, which it was still within my power to do. His father told me that if I exceeded my authority he would get me into trouble.

This again was a method used by suspects to divert attention away from their criminal behaviour but which seldom worked. I remained wholly confident in what I was doing.

After first shuffling around with his hand in between his and his father's seat, probably to hide the knife, the youth left the car. I then searched him but of course nothing was found.

Bearing in mind what the father had just said, I then asked if they would now like to attend the police station with me right at that moment to make their complaint to someone of a more senior rank. They seemed to think this was a very good idea, so they enthusiastically agreed to come with me.

The remaining youths who were part of the same group had closed-in behind me. So I turned and asked if they too would like to support their friends in making this complaint. With an instant display of excited anticipation, they also said they would come along, so I suggested they all followed me in their own transport.

With just a twinge of smug satisfaction I drove from the scene at a steady pace, with them in a variety of cars and motor cycles, following close behind in a lengthy column. I made my way back to the small police office which was a distance of about nine miles away in my own village.

The hill-top village was immediately restored to a state of blissful calm and with a more appropriate atmosphere for the other lads to leave their party and return safely home.

When we arrived at the police office just after 1.30 in the morning, I drove into the yard, whilst everyone else parked along the grass verge.

I first invited the father and his son into the office, where in a calm and controlled environment I was able to take their personal details. I then went outside and told the group that I needed to speak to just one more person. I walked up to the largest of them who had also been the most threatening and obstructive earlier on at the scene of the disturbance. I told him that he seemed the most intelligent so I invited him to join his friend in the office, which he did.

I took his full personal details too and reported them both for using abusive and threatening behaviour in a public place, which included the stream of unintelligible nonsense that was part of their response when I first tried to restore some sort of order in the street.

I then suggested that they returned to their respective homes but they reminded me about the complaint they wished to make. I told them they could come back in the morning, for, as they could see at this very moment I was entirely on my own.

They and their friends then instantly dispersed without any further problem. In the morning, in the cool light of day, they realised they had no grounds whatsoever for making any complaint.

They both received maximum fines in court the following week, under a local bye law which although not severe served adequately to cover the misbehaviour with the knife.

Short term distractions

Having to be fairly combative and focused so much of the time could be quite wearing. For everyone's sake there was a need to try and find a balance that made for a more relaxed disposition.

When opportunities came to savour a few less challenging diversions they were genuinely appreciated and really enjoyed.

A taste of adventure

Over a period of several years, I helped take youths from the local secondary school on adventure walking trips each spring time up into the mountains, either to Snowdon or the Lake District. These were very memorable experiences, particularly as many of the boys had never even seen a mountain before.

It was a very useful exercise in many aspects of character building, and adventure with safety, hard work and determination, team work, planning, mutual support, friendship and fun. We always had lots of incidents to talk about after every expedition.

Upon returning to our village, the experience of sharing so many challenges together in testing circumstances helped everyone to respect and value each other more.

Brian Breacher

In the still small hours

At 2 o'clock one morning and due to the early hour, I quietly drew my car to a halt in the middle of the village. I then just happened to look across to a fire hydrant post about five metres away at the side of the road, and was amazed to see a truly magnificent barn owl perched on top in all its splendid glory. It stayed there just long enough for me to stare in disbelief and wonder at its magical form; before it flew away again, as if in slow motion.

Early rising

On another occasion I was on a regular morning run just before 7 o'clock, through the fertile pastures of the local country estate.

As I reached the top of a hill my breath was quite taken away, not through running but from the sight of a family of foxes, with mother, father and two cubs just over the brow playing happily in the rich green, dewy grass.

Protected badgers

As twilight approached one peaceful evening, I waited with my sons down wind of a badger's sett. After a fairly short period, two large badgers, one following the other, came out of their den just a few yards from where we were standing.

The first shot across the ground into the next field; the second must have heard the faint rustle of our clothes, for it turned around at speed and shot back into its burrow just like a powerful express train.

Apart from giving us quite a start, we regarded this as a sensational experience, and the idea of visiting this particular location had been really worthwhile.

Light relief

Out walking in my own village on another sunny day, I stopped to speak with an elderly widow who was cleaning her windows. "Hello", I asked, "And how are you today?" "I am fine," she replied, "But my arm aches so much it's very difficult when I try to stretch right up to this top window." After checking that no one was looking and in the shelter of a high hedge, I gave her my helmet to hold and cleaned the top window for her, which helped her to smile and I think it quite made her day.

A clean handkerchief

I had just renewed my first aid certificate which had to be kept up-to-date, and I always carried a clean folded handkerchief with me since being spoken to for coughing without using a handkerchief when I was ten years of age, by a rather severe but upstanding disciplinarian who was our church organist at home.

I was walking in the high street of my village, when an anxious and very trusting lorry driver stopped and hurried over to me. "You're just the person I've been looking for," he gasped, full of hope. "I've had something in my eye for a few miles now and it's really beginning to trouble me. I wonder if you could help me please?" I took him to one side out of the wind and asked if he had a matchstick.

He handed me the matchstick and I carefully flicked his eyelid over it, which served to keep a tiny speck of flint exposed in the corner of his eye. I took out my handkerchief, screwed-up a corner and used it to gently remove the foreign body.

I was very pleased and highly relieved that it had worked so well in accordance with the textbook!

The lorry driver blinked, smiled broadly and assured me that he was instantly and pleasantly relieved, and able to continue his journey in complete comfort.

Local gangs

There were one or two gangs living in the villages of the general area where I worked, who sometimes caused mayhem and a great deal of anxiety, even to the more robust of fellow residents.

During this period, I came upon a serious car accident that had taken place just after midnight involving a pregnant mother and her baby. She had been driving towards a bend where there was an overhead railway bridge. At the same time, a nineteen year old youth had been travelling towards the bridge from the other direction - in the process of overtaking another car.

His car struck the pregnant lady's vehicle which then veered into the solid stone bridge wall and threw her out into the unlit road. Her baby ended up alone in the well of the car to the front of the passenger seat. The offending driver did not stop, not even to check or help the lady, but he ran off immediately after the collision.

I waited for the ambulance to take the lady and her baby to hospital. Amazingly the lady suffered only minor injuries as well as shock and the baby was uninjured.

I realised that the offending car belonged to a lad from a nearby village and he was well known to my colleagues and me.

I was also aware that the railway line immediately above where the accident had taken place was routed alongside the edge of the village where he lived, just a matter of four miles away. I made my way there to await his arrival and when I reached this sleepy place a colleague was also waiting for the same youth in connection with another serious crime.

I arranged with my colleague for the offending driver to come to the police station for interview. It was whilst being interviewed there later the same day that he realised he was in serious trouble. Suddenly, he jumped up on to a chair and darted out through a window and ran off. I followed him and caught him just as he was trying to escape on his motor cycle.

I have to admit that I took some pleasure in restraining him and bringing him back into the police station.

A couple of years or so later, the same youth was involved in an even more serious accident on yet another bend, but this time it was he himself who paid the ultimate price.

With the passage of time when they began to have families of their own his pals would have gradually settled down in any event, but this resulted in them reflecting on their behaviour and attitude much sooner, and a safer more relaxed atmosphere was restored for the other residents.

The pensioner looking forward to his holidays

I enjoyed walking to work in the morning because it was refreshing to do so, and I always looked forward to a variety of interesting tasks. It also gave me a chance to speak with people who I enjoyed seeing and offered anyone an opportunity to talk with me in confidence about any of their concerns in which I might be able to assist.

Mr Ewans was already on his garage forecourt and he was a respected engineer who I particularly liked. His whole family was exceptional, and he was a caring and a thoroughly sincere and unpretentious person too; and a very good friend. "Guess what Brian?" he said to me as I approached, "Mr Andrews here had his car battery stolen last night and he is supposed to be going on holiday at the end of the week."

Mr Andrews was retired and he too was another decent kind of person. I told him that I would see what I could do for him. After taking some very brief details I continued to my place of work, but this time in a much more focused frame of mind.

The first part of my plan was to identify a realistic starting point from which the rest of my enquiries could begin to flow. So with due haste I went off to consult the oracle who existed at the hub of village activity and always took a real interest in what was going on in the neighbourhood.

"What do you think Doreen?" I asked her about this problem. "Did you know that Michael, John and Fred are working on a car in the lay-by?" she replied. "I didn't know that but I am really grateful for your help," I said. I was well aware that the lay-by was conveniently close to Mr Andrew's house.

I knew all three lads and was very familiar with their dispositions. I was also aware of where Fred worked and what time he usually came home in the evenings.

I waited for him that very same day and met him as he stepped off the coach. I told him that I urgently needed to speak to him right now; and he accompanied me straight away to my office.

He clearly showed signs of nervousness and at the small police office there was just him and me alone together.

I told him that I needed to talk to him and his friends about the battery taken from Mr Andrew's car. I outlined a picture of what I thought had happened involving the battery, himself and his two pals.

At this stage, I didn't ask whether it was true but I expected him to imagine that I knew it was so. I spoke to him firmly about the need to have the decency and courage to help me return Mr Andrew's battery as soon as was humanly possible. I watched his body language very closely as I focused in on his eyes.

As a result of what I saw, I suspected that the image of what I had just said had struck a chord.

I gave him a few more valid reasons why he needed to tell me the truth about the battery and Fred become even more anxious. He was just at the point where he was taking a deep breath but still wasn't quite sure how to respond, when I said, "I need you to get Mr Andrew's battery for me Fred, right now!"

I then firmly shut the door of the steel cabinet just behind me. "Yes," he said, as he jumped and struggled to catch his breath, "I'll go and get it for you straight away!" This strategy would not have worked without the presence of an underlying conscience or a need to tell the truth, on Fred's part.

So ends the tale of how Mr Andrews and his wife managed to have their car ready for their holiday in good time. The behaviour of the youths involved improved considerably after this experience.

Parents who struggle to cope

Of course, many parents were decent people who were let down by their sons. They struggled to cope with the constant challenges some children presented to them.

On other occasions, it was really frustrating to visit young people at home when their fathers showed no interest whatsoever in hearing what I had to say about the trouble their sons had got themselves into.

High on charm but low on sincerity

I visited the home of a couple in their late twenties to interview the husband and take a written statement from him about a road accident he had witnessed in another county. They seemed to be very secure financially and lived in quite a grand home.

The witness's wife was a lovely person but the husband's body language and voice exposed distinct undertones of insincerity.

It was obvious to me that he was very keen to feign friendship with me for some reason and he duly offered me a cup of coffee which in itself, of course, was not at all suspicious but his overall welcome was simply over-zealous.

It seemed significant that they were new to the area and I wondered why he was working so hard to leave me with the impression that he was such a decent fellow.

His involvement as a witness was altogether innocent but I left their home feeling very uncomfortable about this man.

His wife proved to be a very sweet and genuine soul but I discovered that her family had always been most uncomfortable about her husband's manner and lifestyle.

For a year I became engaged in a period of lone, hair-raising exploits in the early hours collecting data and involved in a great deal of research and enquiry regarding the unusually numerous cars outside his home. I managed to amass enough evidence for him to be arrested and successfully prosecuted for stealing brand new cars from his employer.

I could not help but wonder how many victims were involved, including his own wife! In Court, I overheard him referring to me as a Welsh bastard when speaking to his associates, but in the circumstances I regarded this as a distinct compliment! I particularly enjoyed challenging his solicitor to find any flaw in my evidence, whilst throwing doubt on much of his.

Recognising inconsistencies

A transport company in our village was a well respected concern with a very decent, hardworking manager, staff and drivers. I noticed when walking home late one evening that a very high value car was parked on the driveway of a house that was owned by one of the drivers.

Because I thought it just seemed out of place there, I looked into the car towards the rear seat and noticed it was piled high with a brand of goods that I knew was handled regularly by the local haulage firm.

During the process of dealing with what amounted to be a case of whole scale theft involving just one employee, he admitted that he and other drivers from a variety of different companies regularly swapped goods entrusted to them by their employers.

He had just sold a large quantity of stolen goods to an acquaintance with a Jaguar car, but this was only a small part of the total illegal stock kept in his garage which was recovered during this enquiry.

More thinking time

It was a real privilege to be able to walk around the village and talk with people. It was also a very suitable environment for some creative thinking on how to deal with any outstanding crimes.

This gave me lots of opportunity to make my working life more interesting, whilst keeping a lid on anti-social behaviour which is what I thought it was all about, in addition to earning my keep and justifying my existence. At the same time local people were frequently given some very interesting stories to read in their weekly newspapers.

Powerful reasons versus animal cunning

"I only went to my neighbour's for a few moments and someone stole my radio off the kitchen table," the distressed lady exclaimed as she stopped me when I happened to be passing by; and she had no idea who could have taken it!

I asked whether she was aware of anyone at all who might have called at her home while she was visiting her neighbour. "Well, only Roger the delivery boy with some groceries," she said, "but I know it wouldn't have been him."

Knowing Roger quite well, I didn't visit him straight away but called at his neighbour's home and asked her whether she had seen Roger coming home, just a short time before. She said that she had and I asked whether she had noticed him carrying anything under his jumper. "Well yes, I did as a matter of fact," she said.

Well, that was the easy bit, but the next stage was to decide how and when to approach him. If I spoke to Roger too soon he would panic and probably adopt a defiant attitude. He would be unlikely in those circumstances to tell me where he had temporarily hidden the radio, and I may not find it either. He could well then damage or dispose of it.

If I allowed him to develop a false sense of security, I thought, I could speak to him later on and persuade him more easily to produce the stolen item so that it could be returned to its rightful owner.

I waited a week and then went to his home to see Roger in the presence of his mother. I spent about fifteen minutes outlining a number of significantly credible reasons why he should reflect seriously on his behaviour and have the courage to enable me to return the radio to its owner, who was a very decent person who did not at all deserve to lose the radio.

I eventually managed to persuade him to do just that. He took me to his garden and dug up the radio, which was wrapped in a thick protective plastic bag and he handed it to me. The radio was returned to a very surprised and satisfied resident, and Roger later apologised to her and to his mother.

Good timing

My friend 'the oracle' always seemed to know when the time was right for dealing with a problem and at all times she had the courage of her convictions.

She asked me whether I would handle a situation with extra delicacy, for she suspected that someone was stealing new tyres from his employer and selling them around the village.

She told me who she believed the thief was and where he worked. She also named a lad to whom he had recently delivered four new tyres and who she believed was a person of otherwise good character. The oracle was a very observant, astute and fair-minded woman who would not have wished for other people to suffer as a result of the actions of one very dubious character.

That night I put on my tracksuit and went out in the early hours. I wrote down the details from the suspected stolen tyres which were fitted to a car parked outside the home of a local youth.

In the morning I rang the tyre retailer and asked the owner whether he happened to sell any of this brand of tyre, in particular the four that were marked with the specific registered numbers.

"Well yes I do," he said. "In fact, I have them in stock but none has yet been sold."

I asked what it would mean to him if these very same tyres were being used on a car at the present time in the village where I worked. "Well, I don't know how but if that is so they would no doubt have been stolen from my company." he said, "There is no mistaking that!"

That evening, a couple of miles outside of the village, I stopped the lad with the tyres as he was driving home from work. He confirmed having bought them from the person who I suspected was the thief employed at the tyre company. I took him to a nearby police station where he cooperated and made a written statement to that effect.

Being aware of the disposition of the person who had sold him the tyres, he should have known better, of course. However, I managed to justify accepting his claim that he had not realised they had been stolen and I avoided getting him into trouble.

I then dealt with the dishonest employee for stealing quite a few tyres from his unsuspecting employer.

Under age smoking

I happened by chance to recognise an eighteen year old young man walking through the village. I was very pleasantly surprised to see him, for I recalled that I had taken a packet of ten cigarettes from him four years earlier after seeing him smoking in a street of the last town where I worked. Being a non-smoker myself I had no problem relieving him of the cigarettes.

But I felt that it wasn't for me to dispose of them, so they were always kept in my possession, both at the former and at the present police stations.

I told him that if he could wait just a while I had something for him and I popped into the police station to retrieve his cigarettes. I handed them to him with a smile but suggested that he may think they were no longer suitable for smoking! He thanked me for them and said that he had not smoked since I had taken them from him that day, which was very nice to know.

Chapter 4: Fatal Road Traffic Accidents

In all I dealt with fourteen fatal road accidents, almost all during the time when I was based in my village.

These were always quite challenging and interesting tasks, by virtue of the carnage caused to the thoroughly innocent, whilst the culprit often did his arrogant and cunning best to avoid prosecution. Serious accidents always required very thorough and sensitive handling.

After dealing with the first fatal accident, I realised that if a meticulously detailed series of checks was undertaken, a virtually flawless result could be achieved by the investigator, even though there was always a great deal of bloodshed and chaos to survey when first arriving upon the scene.

Five men died in one car

Possibly the worst accident I ever attended involved five men in one car which was hit head-on by a heavy lorry whose driver had lost control when travelling towards them down a steep hill.

Such was the force of impact and its dramatic effect that all five young men burned to death before they could even attempt to escape from their car.

I can in fact recall all the fatal accidents that I attended, for they were so dramatic and heart-rending.

Informing the next of kin

After once dealing with the first stages of a fatal road accident, I arrived at the home of the deceased. The door was opened by his seven year old daughter who was alone in the house.

I asked if her mummy was there and I was told that she had just left for work; that her daddy had not yet come home and his dinner was ready for him in the oven! I left the child with a kindly neighbour and went to her mum's work. It took a long time to convince her that it was in fact her husband who had been killed and that no mistake had been made; his body had already been identified at the scene by a colleague.

The ripples from this event were already proving to be very painful indeed, so you can only hope that the family would receive all the necessary support they required and deserved.

On a frosty Christmas morning

One quiet, cold Christmas morning at 12.30, I was just making my way home when a driver stopped to tell me there was a body on the main road at the edge of the village.

Within just a few minutes I found an elderly gentleman who had been run over and killed. About twenty minutes later, after celebrating Christmas Eve at a local pub, the relatives of the man arrived on the scene and identified the body.

I collected a few fragments of headlight glass and other debris at the point of impact, then went with the body to the mortuary after death had been certified by a doctor at the roadside.

Later that morning, I returned to have a closer look at the victim and noticed that a very clearly visible imprint of a section of car tyre in clay-like soil had dried up on the side of his face.

I arranged for this evidence to be photographed before visiting his family at lunchtime on Christmas day. Their turkey dinner had been dumped outside with the garden waste and naturally the whole household was extremely distressed.

At the post mortem I watched the pathologist locate a walnut sized tumour lodged between the skull and the brain. This probably explained why in a troubled frame of mind the man had insisted on leaving his family at a local bar to begin his journey home, alone and by foot.

It then seemed that he managed to stumble on the uneven grass verge and fall into the road in the path of oncoming traffic.

I next liaised with colleagues in our Stolen Vehicle Squad to check their vehicle manufacturers' data. I also visited several local car dealers to identify the headlight glass from the glass fragments, and the make of tyre from the tread pattern, so the manufacturer and model of the car could be established.

After this detail was verified just a dozen or so car owners were traced locally and visited, before the damaged suspect car and its driver was successfully traced.

A few men were extremely embarrassed when I visited them because they had not wanted their wives to know where they were on that particular evening, nor who they were with.

They were not where they had said they were, nor were they on their own or with their wives!

There was insufficient reason for taking this case any further beyond speaking with the driver who had unknowingly hit the pedestrian.

Managing the plain awkward

I have a particularly clear recollection of dealing with a gang of criminals who were in two cars racing along the main road from a nearby town to my village, in an indecent hurry to reach the pubs before they shut. The leading car had overtaken a transit van as it was entering a double bend. As it drew alongside the van a mini car came towards it on the same side of the road from the direction of the second bend.

The offending driver, in a desperate attempt to avoid the car, cut in front of the van and mounted the near-side grass verge. At this stage he lost control of his car and swerved back across the road into the oncoming mini car. The result was that the off-side front wing of his car became detached and entered the windscreen of the mini car before piercing the driver's throat and killing her instantly.

She and her passenger were residents of my village and had just returned from their honeymoon in the car they had borrowed from her father. Her husband was thrown many yards away into a deep ditch at the side of the road where he remained motionless as a result of sustaining very serious injuries, mainly to his femur and ribs.

It was dark at the time and passing traffic stopped to help, as you would expect, but the leader of the gang who possessed an objectionable and violent personality, told them to "f... off," if they knew what was good for them.

Fortunately they ignored this uncouth individual, as any right minded people would.

I arrived within a few minutes and began the process of examining the scene and recording every detail. Before I left, the brothers of the injured husband arrived in an understandably agitated and distressed state. They told me that if I left these thugs to them they would deal with them appropriately, and being sturdy farmers they were more than capable of doing just that. I had to assure them that this was something I must be left to get on with to the best of my ability, without that kind of help.

I then accompanied the body to the mortuary, so that when I attended the post mortem the next day I could ensure that the body being examined was the one taken from the scene of this particular accident.

My role at the mortuary when the pathologist examined the body, aside from one of identification, was to ensure that the evaluation of the injuries was consistent with what I knew had happened at the scene.

I next visited the hospital where the driver of the offending car and his passengers were being treated for minor injuries.

When I arrived, the surly 'leader' of the gang stuck his chest into mine in an attempt to intimidate me. Not only was he a pathetic individual, but to be threatened by someone like him would make anyone even more determined to achieve a just and successful conclusion. In any event the prospect of fear or intimidation should never cause you to become distracted.

I told the 'gang' that I would need a statement from each of them but in typically belligerent fashion they said that none of them had seen anything of any evidential value.

I politely assured them that a negative statement would be fine if that's what they wished. I wrote down what each had to say, especially the reasons why they claimed to have seen nothing of significance at any time leading up to the accident, and then made sure that every document was signed.

The benefit of this course of action became obvious at the trial. As each of the five hostile witnesses entered the witness box fully prepared to support the defendant on behalf of the defence, each of their signed statements was produced by the prosecution. This was followed by the judge directing them in turn to leave the witness box, without giving any evidence whatsoever.

Evidence of marks found at the scene and of impact damage was particularly crucial to the prosecution case.

The driver was found guilty of causing death by dangerous driving and sent to jail - for a mere three months, and disqualified from driving for fifteen years! I cannot recall any mitigating circumstances that would have justified such a puny sentence being passed on this unashamed individual.

Of course, the life of the surviving passenger was completely shattered and sadly he died not many years later.

The emotional impact

Although each of the fourteen fatal accidents I attended were horror stories in their own right, I was rarely affected by them emotionally as there was such a need to concentrate and absorb all the vital detail within a limited available time span.

I can recall just one occasion when the shivers briefly ran down my spine. This occurred soon after I had attended a post mortem following a fatal road accident.

I visited a local restaurant for lunch and it was not until I had almost finished the meal when I realised that liver and bacon hadn't been such a sensible choice to have made after all!

I always enjoyed putting the files together, during which time it was essential to keep in mind all the tactically distracting questions the defence was likely to employ. This forthcoming challenge stayed on my mind right up until completion in Court but the experience was always quite satisfying.

Chapter 5: Time For a Change

I was informed by someone with a sense of humour, that the small disruptive element in my village had put the flags out soon after I left! The truth was that I maintained contact with many people there and I still visit the village right up to this day.

In fact after I was promoted Mr Ewans and his wife drove over 120 miles to say hello! I was overwhelmed by what they did and really thrilled to keep in touch with them.

Murder enquiry

For six months in 1965 I was involved in an enquiry into a murder that took place on a small country footpath at the edge of a medium sized community. The main thrust of the enquiry involved a series of carefully detailed and painstaking checks and counter-checks, in which I thoroughly enjoyed being involved.

The movements, behaviour and habits of so many adults living within, visiting and passing through the community was so systematically and meticulously investigated, that all manner of perversions and misbehaviour came to light.

Many, many lies told by quite a few interviewees were necessarily uncovered, through counter checking what they had said, then checking again and re-checking until the truth, which was often very sordid, eventually came to light. There was no escape for anyone who chose not to tell the truth. The murderer was identified after just over a six month period of investigation.

At the end of each sixteen hour day a colleague and I went on a five mile run to refresh ourselves after sitting down for almost all of the day, checking the paperwork of investigators for anomalies or inconsistencies.

Outward Bound

After the murder enquiry, I was seconded for a month on an Outward Bound Course as a temporary instructor, at Burghead in Scotland.

This was a brilliant form of light relief involving running, orienteering, fitness training around a series of sand hills; sailing in dipping lugs, hill-climbing, severe grade rock-climbing and abseiling.

On a day of mountain trekking in Glen Affric, which our Watch (Naval terms were used) entered alongside a fast flowing burn, the scenery was stunning and the colours were exhilarating. We saw a herd of magnificent red deer grazing on the spring-time slopes, as we walked off into the distant mist up and over a heavily snow covered mountain, crossing several crevices en route.

Interestingly, the Watch leader for one of the teams of young people was normally resident in a Borstal (Correction) Institution, whilst one of his charges and peers was a young prince from Saudi Arabia.

The youth responded extremely well to the challenge of leadership and he established himself as a strong and worthy captain.

The ethos of the course involved hard work alongside physical and mental challenge with endurance, as a means of building character. Firm and measured direction throughout the whole Course, at all levels, was therefore extremely important.

Those entrusted with the responsibilities of leadership, had the opportunity to discover qualities within themselves that they probably never knew existed. The youth's confidence noticeably blossomed through being chosen as a leader; and his energy, common sense and example were inspirational. It became clear that the young prince was impressed by this person's qualities and I believe that he and the Watch leader became very good friends.

They may well have recognised a kindred spirit in each other, for both were under considerable pressure to perform well, due to the expectations of others.

I am certain that the young Watch leader's experiences there proved to be a catalyst for change in his life.

Chapter 6: Working With Young People

Cadet training

When I was about thirty years of age I was at my fittest and had the privilege of training 16 – 18 year old cadets who wished to join the police force at 19, (they don't have paid cadets any more). They were all well-motivated and I was responsible for training them in fitness, adventure and community service; and helping to run their residential courses.

They were trained to a high standard and were entered into a variety of competitions, such as non-stop fifty-mile hill-walking races in the Long Mynd in Shropshire; long-distance (125 mile Devizes to Westminster) canoe races; the Ten Tors annual winter race on Dartmoor, and so on.

They were sent on Sail Training (tall ships) and outward- bound, canoeing and life-saving courses; and a number of adventures that combined rock-climbing as well as sailing.

They also were seconded to a variety of Cheshire Homes, Hospices and other establishments where total care was required for people across the age groups. I was amazed how they approached these tasks with such calm maturity and returned afterwards having benefited greatly from the whole interactive experience of caring and giving.

The Cadet Training Centre was also authorised to run The Duke of Edinburgh's Award Scheme in its own right, which meant that I ran this very worthy Scheme and its associated activities. It was commonplace at cadet passing-out parades for parents to remark on how their sons and daughters had changed, with their confidence zooming upwards after only a very short time.

A lack of leadership and hope

For a period of about two years, I was engaged in yet another thoroughly worthwhile and interesting job, to recommend proceedings or otherwise for all the young people aged 10 – 17 years in a medium-sized town and the wider rural area, who had become involved in breaking the law.

This entailed making background enquiries with social workers, head teachers, parents and any other people I believed could make a useful contribution to my enquiries, such as the family GP.

This responsibility enabled me to see the problem from other points of view, especially when I was able, at first hand, to observe the young person's situation at home. I became very familiar with some of the hopeless domestic circumstances in which many young people struggled to exist.

I came to the conclusion that this was a very useful way to understand young people who fell foul of the law and who almost always lived either in really uninspiring circumstances, or had something about their personal history that explained the reason for their behaviour. This was a privileged position which enabled me to make reasoned and balanced decisions as to what should happen to each young person.

It was in their interests for parents to share their problems with me, because I needed to know enough about their circumstances to make an appropriate decision.

I was surprised by a few professional people who knew so little about their children's strengths and weaknesses, interests and hobbies, that they were unable to make any worthwhile contribution to this decision-making process.

The child who found his mother murdered

I interviewed two young lads who lived in a Children's Home and had been caught shoplifting after already appearing in Court for a similar matter on a previous occasion. The first one had ended up in Care after coming home from school to find his mother lying dead behind the toilet door, having been murdered by his father.

The second lad was there because his mother had died and his father was frequently being arrested for interfering with women.

The Children's Home staff, who happened to be extremely caring people, took much of the blame due to a brief lapse in supervision as a result of a shortage of staff.

I had no hesitation in recommending that no further action be taken against these young people – and what an easy decision that was to make!

Non-accidental injuries

For a couple of years I represented a police district at non-accidental injury, multi-agency case conferences, involving the medical profession, education and social services, the police and others. These were held whenever babies, children or young people were found to have been injured in suspicious circumstances, or abused at home or elsewhere.

Almost all were high-profile cases and, according to the circumstances, it would usually be deemed practicable for one single agency to take appropriate action on behalf of the whole conference. Whenever the police agreed to undertake the responsibility, the others generally had little idea of what that would in practice entail, or how the objective would be achieved. This sometimes led to a lack of understanding as to why a particular course of action was taken.

The same problem also applied to whichever other agency was required to take the initiative, for even at the highest level of multi-agency activity communication could be woefully inadequate; and an appreciation of each other's roles was often quite limited.

Subsequent improvements involved the primary agency being required, at the outset, to ensure that their multi-agency colleagues had a very clear grasp of what exactly they would be doing and how and why.

Just before I left the area, I wrote a paper to ensure that continuity would have every chance of surviving after I handed over the role to a colleague, and he would not have to start again right from the beginning. A healthy free flow of ideas and information between agencies, or even within them, did not always seem to exist. Even if you had put yourself out to win over certain key individuals so that a reasonable level of cooperation existed, it was still far from guaranteed.

Problems sometimes occurred through the reluctance of individuals to share essential items of information. This seemed especially odd as we were all supposed to be working towards improving, encouraging and promoting the welfare interests of all young people in the same geographical area. In any event, it was healthy to constantly seek to improve professional standards within the community as a whole. It occurred to me that a more free-flowing exchange of vital information would have helped everyone involved to advance their contribution to the overall service at a similar pace.

Some individuals appeared to take the view that if they managed to keep their experiences and awareness to themselves, they would be seen in a better light than their colleagues. This seemed to be a cultural problem that existed due to a lack of interactive generosity or community spirit. Mutual support and cooperation did not always occur instinctively with everyone in the public services. It is just as well that there were many exceptions to this trend.

The ten year old boy I met

One quiet Sunday morning I stopped to speak with a ten year old lad who was walking along the main shopping street of a small town. He was carrying a large bucket filled with hot water, with cloth, scrubbing brush and soap and he appeared a little uncomfortable with his heavy load.

I gently enquired as to where he was heading and he told me he was going to the local cemetery about a mile away, to give his mother's grave its annual Easter scrub.

This was a regular custom for people who also liked to brighten and adorn their family graves with fresh and colourful spring flowers at this time of year. When I asked how he felt about having to scrub the grave he assured me that he was comfortable with the task itself

He added that the problem was that he did not want to be seen by his friends, for he would then have to explain where he was going and what he was going to do.

He said that his pals were very loyal friends and from decent families. But each had both a mother and father, which meant they could not be expected to fully understand his situation at this moment in time. Neither did he wish to enlarge on something that to him was so very, very personal.

He assured me that once he had finished cleaning - the weeding, scrubbing, and washing the small marble chips, he particularly enjoyed being in the top corner of the cemetery where the grave was situated.

This gave him the opportunity to spend some time alone with his mother and grandmother, which always induced a very special, warm and cosy feeling within him. He assured me that only they would know exactly how he was feeling and what he would be thinking about them.

He told me he did not actually know what his mother looked like, for he had never seen a picture of her – and had been only two years of age when she died. He said that he remembered his grandmother with great affection, because she had been particularly kind to him and had not passed away until he was seven.

I next spoke with him almost a year afterwards, when I found him looking particularly sad and deep in thought. He said that earlier the same day the aunt with whom he lived had gone and drowned his dog! He told me that upon arriving home from school he had opened the door to see his dog just inside. It was dead and still floating in a tub of water. The tub was covered with a piece of corrugated zinc with stones on top to ensure his dog was kept down in the water.

His aunt, who was his mother's sister, had been there calmly knitting beside the fire in the same room, callously awaiting his arrival home.

He told me that because he was accustomed to his aunt punching him, as well as his two older sisters, every day he was not really surprised. He explained that he had avoided showing any discernible emotion, for he did not want to give her the benefit of added satisfaction.

His domestic circumstances were not known to his teachers and he clearly regretted not having a suitable adult in his life to whom he could off-load a number of personal issues. Most of his teachers, he told me, were really inspiring and he enjoyed being with them.

I realised that his welfare interests were paramount, but he remained adamant that he did not want me to speak to his aunt, because he and his sisters did not like the idea of going to a children's home, which was an option they were threatened with periodically; and they really loved their dad.

He assured me that the people in his Church and Sports Clubs, his Scout group leaders, as well as others - including his neighbours, were always particularly kind and supportive towards him. He actually regarded himself as extremely fortunate to be part of such a very special community.

He made me distinctly aware of how important it is to live within a mutually caring community, which promotes high ideals, worthy values and has ample role models.

I next saw this lad a couple of months later, when I attended a road accident on the town's busy main street. He had been riding down a steep hill on his bicycle towards the main road, when his brakes failed and he began to gather speed.

As he neared the 'T' junction at the bottom, he was heading at increasing speed directly towards the plate glass window of a shop opposite.

Then, just as he was about to reach the main road, a 'bus came across his path. He collided with its rear wheel, which spun him upwards into a backward somersault, and he landed in a heap on top of his bike. Consequently, his thigh was badly bruised, but luckily that was the sole extent of his injuries.

The bus driver emerged from his bus with clipboard in hand to record details of what the lad had to say for himself. Luckily this was generally a caring town where the women were tough and outspoken; and two of them immediately came from their homes to the lad's aid and told the driver to "clear off," which he promptly did!

I arrived on foot, within just a few minutes, to find the slightly distressed lad being comforted. I walked with him to his home about 350 yards from the scene, to ensure there was someone present who would look after him and understand that no-one was to blame.

The only person at home was his aunt, and I was instantly aware that she was a surly individual who showed no sympathy whatsoever for what had happened to this lad.

In fact, now that we were in his home he was far more uncomfortable, as his aunt stood there with arms folded, completely unmoved and glaring quite menacingly at the youth, whose name was David.

I stayed there for as long as I could, to provide him with some degree of moral support, and I tried to make sure the woman understood that he was in no way to blame for the accident.

The dark atmosphere in this house made me feel very anxious and it was odd that everyone had shown concern for the boy except the woman in his very own home.

I managed to speak with David outside in the street a few days later and I invited him to visit the police station club so that we could play badminton or snooker and, if he wished, he would have the chance to off-load some of his concerns.

He came with me and we talked at length about his hopes and dreams for the future; and especially how he might turn his home experiences into something positive. He was usually anxious not to stop for too long, as he always had lots of chores waiting for him at home. We met several times and he always seemed pleased to be given a window into a different kind of world.

At the age of seventeen he left the town, and just a few years later I saw him on the television in the uniform of the Brigade of Guards. He had been chosen to escort the Queen's Colour during a very important State visit.

About six years afterwards I was with a friend when I saw David in a local store during a fleeting visit he was making to the town. We caught each other's eyes and he came straight over, and as we shook hands, I said, "Hello David, you're looking really smart!"

He beamed at me and replied, "I am like this because of you, for you changed my life for me."

As we parted company again, I felt a distinct surge of emotion rushing down my spine, for I suspected that some defining moment had made him realise he could choose to be the person he wanted to be - and the fruits of his endeavours to dignify his life were now quite apparent.

Chapter 7: The Next Phase of My Adventures – and More Challenges

A novel arrest

A colleague and I were just responding to a telephone call from a woman who had seen two men breaking into a neighbour's home. Then a second call soon afterwards said the two men had been seen again, this time leaving with arms full of electrical goods!

I was already on my way after the first call and as I drove into the street from one direction a colleague came in from the opposite end.

I saw the two men running away; the closest to me was crossing a neatly manicured front lawn not far away from the house that had been burgled. I stopped my car and brought him down on the soft grass, which was very convenient for me.

The lady of the house came to ask if I needed any help, which was very kind of her. I realised he had been drinking, so I tied the man's boot laces together very tightly and left him sitting on the lawn.

I then chased after the second burglar and as I gained on him my colleague came around the corner and the thief ran neatly into his arms. The first thief had given up trying to untie his boot laces and was still sitting down, waiting to be collected!

The lady was quite amused and I think she enjoyed the moment's entertainment. Both men were habitual thieves, and drunkards.

The customer in the dirty Mackintosh

Things are not always what they seem to be, as a colleague once discovered when directed to a unisex hairdressing salon after a middle-aged man with a soiled raincoat had called there for a haircut.

The customer had patiently waited his turn until he was invited to sit in the hairdresser's chair. After placing a dust cover around him and ensuring that he was comfortable, the young and attractive hairdresser turned away to pick up her hand- brush.

But as soon as she returned to the customer, she was aghast to see to his front just beneath the dust cover, that there was a great deal of suspicious movement!

She was extremely alarmed, not to mention indignant about what she assumed was happening; so she lifted up the heavy hand-brush and brought it down upon him with a thundering whack – causing him a great deal of pain!

She managed to fracture his finger as well as break his glasses; and he was extremely puzzled to know why she had so suddenly and manically attacked him, whilst he had quite innocently and properly only just begun to clean his spectacles!

She could have been arrested for causing criminal damage and actual bodily harm but, luckily for her, he kindly accepted her embarrassed explanation, together with an apology and the cost of the spectacles. The matter was never taken before the Court but had it done so I am certain that this story would, justifiably in this case, have made it to The News of the World.

Big boys' games

In the early hours one morning, Accident and Emergency staff at the local hospital rang to say that a man had just been admitted with a bullet hole in his head, but they were unaware of the circumstances. He lived in an idyllic village and I hastened to meet five of my colleagues on the outskirts. Although it was about 2 in the morning, from a safe distance we could clearly see the local pub, situated on a prominent hill.

Most unusually, whilst all around was in darkness, it was ablaze with lights and the front door was wide open.

We emptied our pockets of all noisy metal and took off our shoes. We approached the public house, not knowing what we were likely to discover but well aware of the possibility that someone was there with a gun, waiting for us - or not.

We surrounded the premises and slowly approached to see what we could find. There was no-one around on the spacious ground floor at least, so I entered through the front door with a couple of colleagues.

As we approached the centre of the room, we could see that a distinctive pool of fresh blood was lying thick on the highly polished mahogany-topped bar.

Through the force of its own surface tension, the blood was contained within a large, speech-like bubble.

On the carpet just below the blood, was a used .9mm calibre bullet case, which we all realised could certainly have told a very interesting story, the facts of which it was our task to uncover.

I decided to go up the stairs via a narrow stairway in the private quarters to the rear. I crept halfway up, to a point where I began to smell the unmistakable odour of dog and assumed there was a large animal somewhere upstairs.

I straightaway came down with just a little more urgency than I went up. Around the corner I found a huge dog bowl and came to the conclusion that there was indeed a very large hound somewhere up the stairs.

We decided to contain the building by surrounding it until whoever was there emerged, hopefully sober and without a gun, so that he or she could be spoken to!

At 6.30 am a man came to a front bedroom window and I indicated for him to meet us in the hallway below the stairs just inside the front door, which he immediately did. He was the licensee of the premises and was arrested on suspicion of possessing a firearm without a licence.

We then met his dog, which was a large but very friendly Afghan hound.

We took the licensee away and gave him the opportunity to enlighten us as to the events that had taken place in the bar that night. At that stage he was not particularly forthcoming, because he had not yet fully thought through his story. Nevertheless, by various means during mid-afternoon, we were able to piece the jigsaw together.

It appeared that after hours the licensee had been playing cards with two customers whilst all three were drinking heavily in the bar. For the thrill of a drunken challenge, they had then begun experimenting with a game of Russian roulette … unfortunately, one of them lost!

The man now in hospital had pulled the trigger himself and shot a hole right through his head, so the doctor said – but luckily he had miraculously survived to tell the tale. The licensee had some quite serious criminal convictions and indeed held no licence for the gun, which was later recovered from the river nearby, having been hidden there by the third man. This was one big-boys' game for which there were no winners, and I suspect that two of the men had been coerced into taking part by the stronger personality of the more street-wise licensee!

Late evening 'entertainment'

I was again on my own in a car in the town centre. I heard over the radio that one of our 19 year old female colleagues was in urgent need of assistance on account of being verbally abused and physically threatened by two men in their early 40s who were well and truly drunk. This had taken place over a period of about one hour in the car park of a busy shopping centre, during late night closing. I happened to be within two minutes' drive, so I went to give assistance.

As I entered the car park I saw the two men. One was tall and staggering about; the other was shorter, stocky and extremely uncouth. The second man was holding the neck of a large bottle of cider, waving it over the head of the young police woman and yelling abuse.

There were lots of men, women and children in the car park, seemingly transfixed by this spectacle.

I parked my car a short distance behind the two men and approached the individual with the bottle, which was still held above his head as he continued to threaten the police woman.

I stood behind him, took the bottle away and handed it to a security officer, who was among the spectators standing passively nearby.

I placed one hand on each of his shoulders and pressed him to the ground. As his legs buckled, his dog with its lead came in between us. I told the police woman to remove the dog and after she did so, I put the man on the ground.

By this time, I noticed that the window of a large shop facing onto the car park was packed with shoppers who seemed to be fascinated by all the action – and there were dozens of faces pressed right up close to the window.

Amazingly, by now there was almost a complete circle of other people around me who were watching closely. Amongst them I noticed two men, one young and one older, whose body language seemed to be telling me that they were ready to help if I needed them. In this scenario, although you need to be firm it is also most important to keep the 'spectators' on side - but this should never be a problem anyway.

As I held the drunk firmly to the ground, his drinking companion lurched towards me through a gap in the crowd, as if to render assistance to his friend. I stuck my foot out towards him and warned him to clear off or I would deal with him too; and he stumbled away without the need for a further warning.

I asked the young police woman to put handcuffs on the drunk who I had by now arrested. She then assisted me in standing him up, prior to walking him backwards to the car. But after we all stood up, he slumped back to the ground in an uncooperative heap.

Not wanting to play games with him or to strain myself lifting up his dead weight, I pulled him easily by the handcuffs along the smooth footpath to our car which was just a matter of a few yards away.

The older spectator then came to help me put him into the rear seat of the car, which I appreciated. The police woman sat in the front passenger seat with the dog and we drove away from the car park.

As we were leaving the car park I kept my eye on our passenger, in the interior mirror. I saw him raise his handcuffed fists above the head of the police woman, so I braked hard and he fell away from her.

I jumped around to kneel on my seat and, as he lunged forward again, I cupped my hand around his chin and threw him back, this time more firmly, into his seat. I warned him against continuing to behave aggressively and he cowered passively in the corner of his seat for the rest of the journey.

At the police station, he was placed in a cell where he continued to bang on the door and shout abuse all evening. But in Court the next day, he made a vexatious claim that I had badly bruised his forearms which he showed to the magistrates.

Placing my fate entirely into the hands of an investigator held no appeal for me, so to protect my own interests I immediately went to the scene of his arrest.

I took a written statement from the security officer to whom I had handed the bottle, and from the owner of a nearby shop. As I expected, they were particularly supportive of my actions and both said they had been very pleased to see me arrive and deal firmly but fairly with the drunken individuals, whose behaviour they and others regarded as quite alarming.

What should have been an elementary and very straightforward investigation, rather pathetically took eleven months to complete even with no proof existing to support the complainant.

It was actually shown, primarily through photographic evidence, that these bruises were the exact size and shape of the tiny circular metal frame of a small window which was about head high in the cell door and against which this drunken man had banged his forearms all evening.

In due course, it was proven that my behaviour towards him had been exemplary. I learned a great deal from this event and became all the stronger for the experience.

Solomon said

There is a very important principle taken from a quote by King Solomon, which says, "He who is first in his own right seemeth just till his neighbour cometh and searcheth him."

This quote deals with drawing conclusions from a one-sided complaint, before the other person has had a chance to speak in his own defence. The theory involved forms the foundational basis for cross-examination. It also highlights the futility and ignorance of gossip, which is commonplace in some of the more basic and rudimentary communities and circles, and which of course makes no sense at all.

Chapter 8: Thinking Ahead

Patterns of limited scope

At 12.30 one morning, I was listening-in on my radio to a commentary from two officers who happened to be close to a store on a town estate when the shop alarm was set off.

Because the officers were nearby, a two-man team of burglars was caught red-handed, as they made a hurried exit from the shop.

The police deal regularly with crime patterns and behaviour, which are of limited identifiable or predictable scope.

The movement and activities of criminals, therefore, have to be anticipated as a general rule through a combination of local knowledge, instinct, insight, experience - and luck.

It immediately crossed my mind that the same store could well be attacked again the following evening but not necessarily by the same people, nor even by their associates.

I told a young officer that he and I would visit the same location within the next couple of hours, to familiarise ourselves with the layout of the land.

We travelled there together and found that, if we went through school grounds at the opposite side of the estate, we could approach the store directly at the front, at a higher level, where we would easily be shielded from view by a hedge. I informed my young colleague that it might also be prudent for us to return again in the early hours the following night.

At 1.15 next morning, we parked our car at the same school and jogged across the field. As we emerged at the front of the store we saw five youths - all involved in breaking into the shop.

The shop keeper had not reset the alarm from the previous night, believing it highly unlikely they would be attacked two nights in succession by yet another group of thieves.

We held a useful vantage point some thirty feet to the front and about fifteen feet above them, so I was able to verify in what way each was involved and to identify exactly what they were doing. I told my colleague to slip away and use his radio to call for back-up, so we would have a much better chance of catching all five youths. I then made sure that our colleagues, who were now waiting nearby, encircled the shop covering every likely exit.

At a given signal I instructed them to converge on the youths and as we ran to the shop, four of the burglars scattered in different directions – each into the arms of an individual officer. The fifth youth, who I happened to be nearest, remained still, just about twenty five yards from where I was standing.

I assumed that, at that vital moment, he had chosen to feign innocence, even though I had already noted clear evidence of his involvement.

Considering the circumstances in which he had been found, he and his solicitor were likely to employ a fairly standard defence: that he had been unable to sleep and had innocently and coincidentally been walking by with no connection whatsoever to the other youths, when he was arrested! And the Court would most likely have given him the benefit of the doubt.

I did not advance any further but stopped and looked away from him for a moment to test his reaction. Sure enough, and probably because he thought I may not have noticed him after all, he then also ran away; but I caught him about two hundred yards down the track. All five youths eventually pleaded guilty in court.

You just have to hope that the impact of being caught would have had a very beneficial influence on all of their future lifestyles. Had they managed to avoid capture, or been found not guilty, the experience of getting away with this crime would probably have given them the confidence and bravado to commit more serious offences. Successful detention would also have allowed all five an opportunity to pause and think about the choices they were making, before they continued any further along this desperate path towards an even more fateful future.

Needless to say, the shop owner was extremely pleased, after being targeted twice in two days, that everyone responsible on both occasions had been instantaneously arrested!

The lady and the gun

When I was the duty Inspector, I was called by my colleagues to a house where a woman's husband had threatened her with a gun because he suspected her of having an affair with another man.

Domestic incidents were commonplace and in degree of seriousness were capable of occurring at any point along the whole spectrum of possibilities, at any time.

In the early hours of the morning I arrived at a neighbour's house directly across the road, where the lady had taken refuge because she was tearful and in such a distressed and anxious state.

She insisted that, during a violent domestic argument, her husband had threatened her with a gun and that he was now probably drunk in the house, still in possession of the gun, and alone with their two young children.

I did my best to assess whether she was sincere, or if she was trying to use the police to exact revenge on her husband. I checked with her and a male family friend who was also present, whether or not they knew for certain that her husband possessed a gun or held a firearms certificate.

They said they had no knowledge of him ever having a gun but could not really say for certain whether he had recently acquired one. They were fairly sure that he had never possessed a firearms certificate. His wife also added that her husband had a very fiery temper!

In assessing the strength of the allegation and the most appropriate course of action to take, I had to guard against taking more notice of her emotional state than of any factual evidence. She might not have seen a real gun at all and the husband may well have been completely innocent.

I also had to resist the desires of my junior colleagues, who I suspected would have liked to have seen me making a dramatic entry to arrest the husband, with most of them involved in some way.

I decided that just I and the sergeant would enter the house, whilst the dog handler and everyone else waited outside. I told them they were only to become involved if in the course of time their assistance was deemed to be absolutely vital.

We went first up the stairs to search the bedrooms and found the children fast asleep in one room and the sound of snoring in another. I decided to leave the children where they were, in case awakening them caused too much disturbance. I quietly opened the door of the other room and saw the husband in bed fast asleep – snoring heavily.

I told the sergeant that we would first check the room for a weapon before awakening the husband.

We did this carefully by searching the cupboards, under and in the bed and elsewhere, but no gun or other weapon was found. We were already aware of a toy gun on the landing floor.

An extraordinary degree of concentration is required when you are involved in solving this kind of problem. Your credibility is especially at risk when investigating a serious allegation, on the word of a third party, when you are unaware of her background or history and she is emotionally distraught, with a possible ulterior motive or even mistaken perception; and you are without any clear means of corroboration.

It is even more fraught when physical action plays a part in the solution in the man's own home; especially if he has no inkling as to why two complete strangers should be in his bedroom in the first place.

You must remain aware of the balance of reasonableness throughout the whole incident, on behalf of everyone involved. There is also a need to safeguard your own personal and professional integrity, as well as the physical well-being of everyone concerned, including your own!

Whilst evaluating your options adrenaline whizzes around your body, which helps keep anxiety or fear completely out of the equation. You must first identify your main objective, and then keep your mind on what needs to be done. The first consideration must be one of safety, but after that you simply do not have the time to enquire into the history of their relationship, so you are never really sure whether the bringing together of husband and wife, in the immediate or longer term, is a realistic objective. You can only be guided by your experience and instinct and by what you identify and surmise as you work your way through the problem.

But in this kind of scenario it so happens that at some critical stage your lips and mouth can become horribly dry!

Accountability for your action always rests with you and no one else and you are bound to do your utmost to effect a satisfactory conclusion; but essentially you are on your own – just you and your conscience.

To dispel the husband's likely sense of injustice when he finds strangers in his bedroom wrestling him to his bed, I was ready to explain the reasons for our actions as soon as he awoke. I was confident that the action we had taken so far was fully justified, as well as what we were about to do.

I told the sergeant to go to the other side of the bed and I turned on the light. I roused the husband and pinned him firmly by his shoulders to the bed.

He was, understandably, verbally aggressive in the extreme, and threatened to break my f...ing legs. I held him down and told him that we were there after receiving a serious allegation that he had threatened his wife with a gun.

It was usual when making an allegation as serious as this, for it to have the effect of calming down the individual. This is exactly what happened as the husband immediately became preoccupied with thoughts about the serious nature of what had just been said; and in all the circumstances how best he might preserve his freedom.

No matter how indignant or aggressive they might initially have been, this approach usually had a distinctly sobering effect upon them, primarily because it is not in their best interests to get too obstreperous with the people who are responsible for closely observing what they say and how they behave.

The allegation I had put to him took away his aggression and I was able to relax a little, so that we could sit him up and place handcuffs on him whilst we continued to talk.

He said to me, "It's Mr Breacher isn't it?" I then recalled that we had met a couple of years earlier when he had sought my advice about the licensing laws at the club which he was involved in running.

I believe this helped him to accept that I could be trusted and that my actions were very likely to have been reasonable. By now he was also well and truly sober.

I then took the opportunity to visit the bathroom for some water which I desperately needed to enable me to carry on talking!

Having placated the husband, I then continued to discuss my options with him. I said that I would consider releasing him so that he could remain in his own home, on condition that he did not cause any further trouble with his wife. He said this would be appreciated, provided the man who was with his wife across the road first returned to his home about twenty miles away.

I removed the handcuffs from him and assured him that I would see that this was done; and we parted on friendly terms.

No gun was ever found, which is not to say that it did not exist somewhere, but I was satisfied that even if there was a gun the husband had by now recognised the folly of his behaviour and the incident had been brought to a reasonable and safe conclusion.

I then cautioned the 'family friend' as to the problem he was creating for this couple. I told him that he needed to be seen by the husband to leave the area via the front door, now, which he did without argument.

After outlining the conversation I'd had with her husband and explaining the reasons for my actions, I suggested to the lady that she should stay where she was for the night and to let me know immediately if any further problem arose the next day. The children were still sleeping peacefully, so they remained where they were as the father was now thinking and behaving far more rationally, assuming there was some truth in the original allegation made against him.

Before leaving the scene, I instructed the dog handler to stay with his dog for about thirty minutes at the top of the street, within sight of the house, in case the husband was tempted to visit the neighbour's home.

I then returned to the police station and wrote an account of the incident both for record purposes and reasons of continuity for the benefit of my colleagues coming on duty after me.

Shortly afterwards and before I had time to think about relaxing, I was called to another incident which involved someone who had gone berserk in his home; but that's another story.

Later the same day, when I returned to work at 2pm I wondered whether there might have been any repercussions from the domestic incident the night before, but thankfully there had been none.

However, I was very pleasantly surprised when the husband and his wife visited the police station together in the afternoon, to thank me for the way I had dealt with their problem!

They said that it had played a large part in helping them to reconcile their differences. This was a very reassuring bonus indeed and left me feeling more than satisfied.

Dealing with disputes over such a period of time enabled me to establish an approach that worked for me:

1. Be emotionally detached

2. Know your subject

3. Set out to achieve a just and even-handed conclusion

4. Treat everyone with respect, consideration and parity

5. Gain the respect, trust and confidence of all parties involved

6. First, aim to achieve a rapport with all parties, so they are placed at ease and on-side

7. Assume a conciliatory, approachable, relaxed, confident and diplomatic demeanour

8. Do not draw conclusions until you have listened to everyone, properly and adequately

9. Adopt an appropriate attitude by combining charm, humour and assertiveness

10. Try to understand what makes the main antagonist tick and keep this in mind

11. Identify any irrelevant factors and bring them to their notice

12. Discover what wrongs were committed, by whom, how and why

13. Gain a precise understanding of all the relevant legal and associated issues involved

14. Endeavour to keep the dialogue balanced, on track and constantly moving forward

15. Be flexible and adaptable and keep to the point

16. Identify any issues common to each party involved

17. Highlight the dilemma of the complainant

18. Give everyone involved ample opportunity to explain their point of view

19. Show that you are trying to understand the position of the accused person

20. Identify any considerations that have been overlooked, and explain why this might be so

21. Gently but firmly point out any discrepancies or inconsistencies – with humour perhaps

22. Quote any similar 'third party' situations that you know were amicably resolved

23. Ask what is thought of this resolution, or any other suggested options

24. Summarise and reinforce the rationale behind this particular conclusion, from all points of view

25. Give credit for arriving at a sensible solution and bringing the problem to an early conclusion

There are different ways of applying altruism

Telephone calls all too frequently occurred typically claiming that, "Mum's ex-boyfriend is on his way over with a pick-axe handle" (or a knife)! Usually, the police arrived speedily at the home and set about listening to and gently reassuring the mother of their ability to protect her.

As soon as the ex-boyfriend appeared on the scene behaving like an enraged gorilla, the police officers would then have to change gear in an instant and physically restrain him, often by putting him on the floor and holding him there until he either calmed down, or was handcuffed and arrested. This was a very frequently recurring scenario.

Sometimes completely different approaches were necessary, such as when once called by neighbours late at night because a couple in their early twenties were heard arguing fiercely and there was concern for the welfare of their baby.

I managed to persuade the husband to see if he could stay the night with friends across the other side of town, so that he would have the opportunity to calm down. When I went to see whether he had managed to rouse his friends, he told me they were not there.

It had begun to rain, so I suggested he walked the three-quarters of a mile back to his home, so he might have time to cool down and engage with this problem in a more agreeable and rational frame of mind.

When he arrived home, the arguing re-commenced and I felt that something more was needed to bring him and his wife together. In his presence, I simply said to his wife, "I am beginning to wonder what sort of mother you are, putting your own baby through all this hassle."

The husband immediately jumped to his wife's defence and glared at me for daring to accuse her of being an inadequate mother. I gently backed off as he put an arm around his wife and the quarrelling instantly ceased!

Briefly making myself the common enemy at that very moment caused them to unite, and I left their home with a wry smile and with every reason to believe they were now just ripe for a cosy reunion.

Dealing with prejudices

I was asked to deal with a letter received from an academic at a local university. He wished to complain about the reckless way a police officer had driven a car in the vicinity of a public demonstration that he had attended many miles away.

The tone of the letter was as hostile as his manner when I rang him to make an appointment to meet him to discuss this matter. He was very damning in what he had to say about the officer's behaviour and displayed incredible prejudice. The crass immaturity he showed as to the value of his 'evidence' was obvious to me, even before I knew any of the details.

As I arrived at his home, I was aware that this encounter would probably become an interesting challenge; and as soon as I met him I realised that I first needed to deal with his arrogance. There is no point in wasting time taking a statement from someone with such strong prejudices, for that would result in so-called evidence being taken that was entirely worthless and a waste of everyone's time.

I was obliged to enable him to understand that his perception of the circumstances had been affected by his narrow-mindedness, and that he ought to recognise the folly of jumping to conclusions.

It is most important to make a connection with such a person from the outset if possible, and basically it was quite clear that he was really an okay person.

As I was invited into his home, I noticed a pair of muddy walking boots in the hall and I straight away led him to tell me about an eight mile walk he had just completed.

I mentioned an annual fifty mile hill-walking race I was due to attend the following week with my sons, which we had completed many times before. So for the first fifteen minutes we talked about the joy and challenges of walking. This helped break down the barriers and secure his confidence in my ability to talk through the complaint with him, and he immediately became relaxed and at ease.

I systematically went through his evidence with him as I wrote down his statement and we explored and evaluated every detail of what he had to say. I easily managed to change his view as to the strength of his evidence and together we concluded that he had in fact very little to say of any evidential value, as would be needed by a Court.

Before I left him, he assured me that he was completely satisfied that there had been no grounds for complaint whatsoever, at least insofar as his view of the incident was concerned, and we parted company on extremely good terms. I quite enjoyed this aspect of my work.

Prepared to repeat anything you say

I learnt in the first year or so of my service, that it should always be a policy of mine not to say anything to anyone that I was not fully prepared to repeat in public...such as in Court. Therefore, I always endeavoured to choose my words very carefully.

I sometimes needed to visit officers who were patrolling the streets, to make sure all was well with them or to see whether they had any concerns or queries. In the early hours one Friday morning, that was exactly what I was doing when I asked two young female officers if everything was okay.

"Well," they said, "we are having a problem with someone who is in his van and appears to be very drunk. We have asked several times but he refuses to unlock his door and we don't know what to do!" "Well, let's go and see, shall we?" I said. He was still at the side of the road just a couple of hundred yards away.

I banged my fist on his door, and shouted firmly, "Hey you, open this f....ng door, now!" He jumped up and opened it straight away. "There you are," I said. "That's how you do it, if you have to. You can deal with him now."

To the naïve or uninitiated, the use of basic Anglo Saxon might seem crude or unacceptable. But it is a better option than taking a chance on someone driving away in his condition and killing someone just a little further along the road.

My actions were much easier to explain than attempting to justify any weakness or short-sightedness to the next-of-kin, or a Coroner's Court, in allowing him to drive off in such a lethal condition. It is also a form of language that some people understand and respond to more readily; and it can be impossible to reason with a drunk.

The secret of managing this kind of situation, once the element of danger or risk to the public or to the person himself has been attended to, is to change channels immediately and treat the suspect with as much respect and propriety as can be mustered.

A workable combination of the three elements of charm, humour and assertiveness are required in every situation, but in different measured proportions. Experience and practise help you to discover what works best for you with any particular person and in any given circumstance.

One thing is certain, if you cannot do charm or humour, or sincerity, you will certainly have a problem, whoever you are.

Two drunken drivers - one car

I happened to be waiting at the roadside one evening when I saw two men walking to a parked car which was then driven away. I did a sort of double take as it struck me that there was an air of indecisiveness about the driver as he approached and opened the door of the car.

The car stopped after a distance of only ten yards or so. The driver got out and staggered around the front of the car. His passenger then left his seat and walked unsteadily to the driver's seat.

After swapping places, they made their way along the street again for just a very short distance of about five yards.

It seemed that it was even more of an effort for the second person to drive, so they exchanged seats again and the first driver eventually drove off down the road.

Whilst their actions could be seen as quite funny, the situation was also serious enough for me to do something about it, especially before anyone got hurt since there was lots of traffic in the area. I stopped them a few hundred yards down the road and arrested both men for driving the same car after drinking too much alcohol.

I don't know why they drank so much that evening but I had to ring the first driver's mother who came a long way from the south coast to collect his possessions and take him home.

She was such a decent woman that I thought she deserved a full explanation as to why I had no choice but to arrest them both. I believe the driver felt obliged to agree with my decision too.

Her son was also a very pleasant person throughout the whole incident, even though his decisions in the first place were for some reason seriously flawed.

Brian Breacher

Seeking advice when it is needed

About fifteen minutes before officers went out on patrol, it was customary to brief them and assign individual areas of responsibility to them. A young married Scotsman had just joined my team and I believe this was his very first week. At 6 am, I allocated a part of the town to him and told everyone what they should do before commencing their patrols.

They were to undertake some research into their respective areas, to find out whether they could provide any kind of input into the detection of the crimes that had taken place overnight, or even the previous morning, wherever this was at all feasible.

Steve, the Scotsman, came to me a little while later and told me that in the section of town where he was to work that morning, a very large window and lighting at the Council Offices had been smashed sometime in the early hours of the night. In excess of twenty thousand pounds worth of property had been destroyed! "What can I do about this?" he said.

I told him that this would have created a lot of noise and you can rest assured that someone would have heard it. As it occurred at the YMCA end of the shopping area, whoever was responsible could possibly have run across the road towards that accommodation.

His job first of all, was to winkle out the person who got out of bed to see what was going on. Find that person and see what he or she has to say about how many people were seen running away, their ages, gender, their mode and colour of dress, and their direction of travel.

I was involved with the YMCA at the time, so I told him how he could access the block of flats.

Two hours later, Steve came to see me again and told me that he had found a witness and taken details of four youths who had been seen running across the road towards the YMCA, immediately after the crash was heard. "Now, what do I do next?" he said.

"Speak to the manager and see if he can identify the youths; or knock on the doors of a few of the flats and see what you can find out about their identities and whereabouts – and good luck."

Steve was a stocky and fit individual, who had played football for Scottish Youth, so I was very confident that he would have no problem in dealing with these suspects.

Just three quarters of an hour later, he returned and told me that he was walking up the stairs of the YMCA flats when he recognised the four suspect youths who were coming down the steps towards him. He had arrested all four and they were now in the secure custody area. "What do I do next?" he said.

I suggested he carefully chose one of them and questioned him thoroughly; then interview the others in turn and see what they all had to say for themselves. I was confident he would take no nonsense from any of them.

Just two hours later, he returned to me once again and informed me that all had admitted their part in damaging the window and lights and they had been duly charged. This might sound a very straightforward exercise but Steve's modesty, approach and tenacity, without a doubt, would have been key factors in the success of this investigation.

I think Steve was very satisfied with his day's work and he would have learnt a great deal from the experience, as you always do. He was deservedly awarded a commendation for his efforts this day, and his ability and courage went from strength to strength from that time onwards.

The angry boyfriend

I heard on the radio about 1 o'clock in the morning, that an immediate police presence was required at the scene of a violent domestic disturbance which was in progress in what was usually a quiet village. As I was not too far away, I decided that I would attend.

When I reached the scene, another colleague had also arrived in support. The woman was cowering in the lounge of the house that was rented in her name. Her boyfriend had, apparently, returned there after drinking heavily and had lost his temper, causing several hundred pounds' worth of damage. The bath was smashed, several internal plaster walls had holes punched through them, and numerous pieces of furniture had been broken.

In order to decide exactly how I should deal with the man, I asked his lady friend if she wished for him to be charged; for if she did so, she would need to make a written statement as to the circumstances, ownership and her willingness to support Court proceedings.

She said that this was a course of action in which she would not really want to become involved.

I then persuaded him to leave the area for the night and stay elsewhere until he was of a more agreeable disposition. He left immediately while I remained in the house for a short time with my colleague.

I remember we agreed afterwards, with some relief, that this was probably the most peaceful option for us too, on account of his sturdy build and the noticeably thick wrists which he had probably acquired as a result of the physical nature of his work.

It was a month later, when I was again alone in a car just after 1 o'clock in the morning, and another similar request was made for my attendance at the same location, for the same reason.

I remember thinking, 'Here we go again!' And within about twelve minutes I reached the same lady's home as two of my colleagues arrived there also.

The man was in the house on his own and even more damage had been caused inside, for on this occasion he appeared to have gone berserk. I was told that the lady tenant was waiting and being consoled at the home of relatives in the next street.

I left my colleagues with the man, who by now appeared to be calm. I went away and listened to what the very distressed woman had to say. I asked her again whether she wished for her boyfriend to be arrested and she told me that because of his persistent violence towards her and her property, she now was prepared to make a formal statement and assured me that the damaged property belonged to her.

I returned to her home and faced her boyfriend to tell him that he was being arrested for causing criminal damage. He then asked if he could first collect his coat from a bedroom, so I decided that for the sake of a more peaceful exit from the house, it would be prudent to go along with this request.

I was also aware that this is often a ploy used for gaining thinking time in preparation for making a dramatic escape. Or he might even choose to lock himself in the bedroom or the bathroom, so I accompanied him upstairs following him very closely.

I stood in the doorway of the bedroom as he recovered his coat and then followed him back down the stairs. As we were walking down the steps, I had this feeling that at any moment he was about to change into battle mode and anything could happen!

In the hall, as he squared up to me, I felt the need to remind the man once more that he was being arrested for causing criminal damage. As I did so, he clenched his fist and drew it back, but before he could throw his punch at me I was obliged to strike him firmly, to restrain him and avoid being attacked by him.

I had taken the view a long time ago, that I could not do my job lying on my back and I did not take kindly to being assaulted.

He fell to the floor and I and my colleagues pinned him down on the ground, where he was handcuffed. We carried him bodily, I behind his head holding his shoulders and my colleagues carrying a leg each. On the way to the front door one of them asked, "Does anyone want a wish?" I promptly told him to shut up – although I did think that it was a very amusing aside!

We placed him in a waiting transit van and took him to the police station. By the morning he had sobered up so he was appropriately charged. Apart from the sympathy I had for his girlfriend, I otherwise quite liked the man when he was sober; for he was a hardworking and tough individual who too often let the demon drink get the better of him.

He seemed to hold no ill-feeling towards me and I certainly had none at all against him.

It was useful to have been involved in a certain amount of competitive sport, for this makes you realise that you should never underestimate the opposition, nor assume that you are better than him, or ever feel any animosity towards your opponent.

When you are obliged to confront a violent person you have to be very cautious. You have to judge for yourself the rights and wrongs of what needs to be done at the time, often in a split second – assuming you are given any chance at all. People who have never had to deal with this kind of hair-raising experience tend to be very quick to criticise the use of firm defensive measures. They can display incredible naivety as well as a tendency towards double standards.

For example, people who witness something for themselves, particularly if they are the victim, may understand that drastic measures needed to have been taken in light of the real threat involved. But when listening to an explanation given after the event involving someone else, they may take an opposite view, especially if their prejudices are aroused in some way.

Just to put things in perspective, the need to take such drastic measures as I have described averaged only once in every six years for me, and I was thankful it did not happen more frequently. In circumstances such as these, you get used to your behaviour being very closely scrutinised.

People resort to a variety of devices to try and put you off course when investigating crime; and there are hazards concerning individual perception, including your own, which must be taken into account.

There is psychological set or expectancy - where a witness sees part of a situation with which he is familiar, then goes on to assume the rest, perhaps inaccurately. There is self-righteousness and feigned sincerity and your own vulnerability to all manner of accusations and duplicity. Many risks are involved when attempting to establish the truth of any situation.

My first duty in this last case was to find a way of protecting the lady, in the long term as well as in the short term; and to secure justice and security for her future through bringing the violent aggressor to account, bearing in mind that he had already shown himself to be persistently unstable.

All of your actions must be justified within the law; and be effective, swift, well-timed and proportionate.

Generally, the person being confronted is the only witness in a position to read all the warning signs and to interpret them as an immediate threat, or otherwise. Such as: the closeness and stance of the assailant, the animated look, the sudden raised eyebrows and widening of the eyes, the clenching of the fist, the stiffening of the sinews, the expanding of his chest, followed by the drawing-back of the arm, and so on.

It is also a fact that if you allow your opponent to take the initiative his confidence will rapidly improve and you can lose momentum as the antagonist finds himself in the ascendancy.

In this case, the boyfriend needed to be arrested, but my own survival became the first requirement in this process. As soon as I was aware that he was just about to take a swing at me, I was compelled to take the initiative - which was both my responsibility and my legal entitlement. The alternative was to risk failing this very distressed woman and leaving her in an even more perplexed, distraught and hopeless state.

To have reacted other than swiftly and firmly could also have been suicidal, because some of these characters when enraged can be really powerful; and enough damage had already been caused.

It would also be pathetically weak not to have had the confidence to deal decisively with such an aggressive bully, in a way that he would understand,

and which afterwards could be justified openly in Court, with all the necessary self-assurance and accuracy.

You must often operate instinctively and perhaps in a way that only you and the victim can ever fully appreciate, simply because you have both seen the aggressor's behaviour - in the raw.

Rarely do you ever have time to pause and reflect on the minutiae of what you might be asked in the sterile and somewhat distanced atmosphere of a Court, where the unscripted and emotive practicalities often clash with the more precise, calm and considered formalities.

That is what the British public seem to prefer; and they always want to support the underdog, which is okay as long as they are in possession of sufficient information and have the wisdom to recognise who the victim really is.

You generally cope anyway, provided you have given sufficient thought to the anticipated line of questioning beforehand; and the situation makes for a very exciting challenge and usually a great deal of satisfaction.

About ten years later, when I undertook some research into the effectiveness of different forms of police action at domestic incidents, the same lady told me that her family was thrilled to have seen this man being carried out from her home into the transit van; and he never ever bothered her again.

This positive action worked well for her, but I am not so sure that individual officers ought to be expected to take this kind of risk without clear legal support!

Better than the TV

In the early hours of the morning a male and a female officer attended a car alarm in a small town on the outskirts of the city. This led them to where a large group of mainly male youths had gathered in a terraced house for a drunken spree, which had spilled out into the street. The youths were mostly drunk as well as hyped-up and aggressive.

Two of their associates were arrested for breaking into the car, which led to several youths attempting to release them by attacking the two officers in the police van.

I heard on my radio that several colleagues had been sent to assist and I made my way there too. Upon arrival I saw the kind of scene that I had never ever witnessed before.

Brian Breacher

Many of the residents were standing on their doorsteps applauding the attendance of the police, as we arrived like the cavalry! Apparently the residents' frustration had reached its peak, due to a series of drunken parties that had been hosted in the same house.

I arrested two aggressive women soon after I arrived, before the youths retreated back into the terraced house; and I could see through the window that it was packed with angry people in the 20 – 30 age range.

I spoke to my colleagues and asked if everyone who deserved to be arrested had been detained and I was told that they had, except for one who was currently in the house and who had severely kicked one of the officers.

Some of the lads in the house then shouted through the window to ask if they could leave and be allowed to go home in peace. I assured them that they could and told my colleagues to be discreet when they were ready to arrest the one remaining youth.

I then moved away to outside a nearby house where about six residents were discussing their concerns over the frequent drunken behaviour of these youths. I joined them to reassure them and said that they were all just about to go home and the situation should now improve.

Moments later, I saw one lone youth walking away from my colleagues towards where I was standing in a semi-circle of people, near the open doorway of a house which happened to have two large stone steps at its entrance. He was being discreetly followed by a few officers and I noticed his pace begin to quicken. I realised that this must be the individual my colleagues had been waiting for.

It was likely he was just about to merge with the group of people I was talking to, in the hope that he would look less conspicuous. I thought he would then attempt to escape through the open doorway of the house and, as he was about 6' 4" tall, he was certain to cause mayhem and damage.

I waited for the moment when he would make his move; and as I suddenly saw him make a dash for the open door, I followed him. In one stride he cleared the two steps to enter the hall of the house. I dived over them and brought him down by tackling him mid-way around his legs. We both fell with an almighty thud into the hallway with me landing on top of him.

As I did so, four of my colleagues jumped over me and handcuffed him before lifting him up bodily.

They carried him back out into the street, all within ten to fifteen seconds and placed him in the waiting transit van.

He was so winded that he had to be taken to hospital for treatment but thankfully nothing more serious was wrong; and no damage was caused in the house. As he was taken away, the owner of the house said to me, "That was far better than anything I have ever seen on the television!" We then left the area assured that everything was returning to a peaceful state.

Between the devil and the deep blue sea

I was driving around the town with a colleague about midnight when we and other officers were sent to a council house.

A gang of drunken individuals with a pickaxe handle and brandishing a shotgun had gate crashed a happy partying household after breaking down the door and discharging the firearm!

Several cars were directed there, so I and my colleague chose to approach from across a footbridge close to the rear of the house. As we left our car, we saw a youth running over the bridge towards us carrying an extra-large rolling pin. I asked him where he thought he was going with that! He told me he was looking for the guys who had invaded their party. I had just relieved him of the rolling pin, when I was contacted by radio and told that the person with the shotgun had been seen in the city centre, nearby.

This placed me in a predicament, because we had no time to take the arrested youth to the police station and it would not have been safe for him to come with us.

We were in quite a remote area, so I decided to handcuff him to a convenient lamp post and collect him later. We left him attached to the street lamp and went to assist in the search for the gunman with the help of a dog and his handler who were already on the scene.

Within about ten or so minutes the man with the gun was found hiding in a hedge, and arrested.

After ensuring that no further assistance was needed at the centre, I suddenly remembered the lad at the lamp post, so I and my colleague returned there with all due haste.

I was relieved to find that he was still happily awaiting our return. All in all, I felt that he had been a good sport, so we released him with a gentle caution and he seemed very relieved that he had managed to avoid being taken to the police station.

The specimen bottle

I had no choice but to arrest a man early one evening after he had become so irritated by his neighbour that he had rammed a milk crate through his glass-fronted door. I took him to the police station and he waited in an annex until a drunken driver in a separate incident had provided a specimen of urine.

I eventually moved the irate man to a room known as 'the surgery' as it was used for medical examinations, for he had cut himself and was awaiting the attendance of a doctor. The prisoner was very hyped up and belligerent. After sitting down for a brief moment, he jumped up and took hold of the urine specimen bottle the previous prisoner had used. He placed it under the tap and began to fill it with cold water.

I said to him, "Someone has urinated in that!" Disbelievingly he replied, "Yeah."

He then carried on filling it with water before putting it to his lips. He obviously had not heard or understood me the first time, so again I told him that someone had peed in that bottle! But again he ignored my warning and carried on drinking all of the contents. Then in an immature show of defiance he even licked his lips afterwards!

Although the variety, frequency and the nature of what people did never ceased to amaze you, it was relatively easy to cope with people like this. Some were sad, many let their emotions get the better of them; whilst others were just ordinary folk and very decent at heart, who had got themselves into a spot of bother that they regretted.

Many situations were also quite amusing and you definitely needed to keep a sense of humour for most of the time.

Chapter 9: History, Human Nature and Spirituality

There were many moments when my work allowed me a few minor flirtations with a less aggressive and challenging world and I had the opportunity to connect with historical events from many centuries past and to meet some fascinating people.

Roman burial

I was called to the scene of a fallen oak tree in horse-racing country on the Berkshire Downs. The tree had keeled over in a gale, to reveal a Roman grave with skeletal remains buried beneath its roots. This made quite an unusual story for the local press, not to mention the owner of the land; and it was extremely interesting for me too.

Mediaeval skeletons

Nearby on yet another occasion, I was called to the edge of a farmer's field which had unexpectedly revealed the site of two mediaeval graves, where two skeletons were unearthed, still lying in clearly identifiable, mediaeval positions.

The archaeologist's report for the local coroner into both of these discoveries made particularly absorbing reading.

Little diamonds

I met a little girl aged about six years, at the home of one of a gang of youths who caused incredible anti-social problems throughout a wide area, on account of the relentless misbehaviour in which they were involved. When I first went to the house to interview her brother, she caught my eye, because she shone like a little diamond.

Much later on, I saw her on a regular television series and realised that she had become a very well known TV star. I became even more convinced that you should never underestimate anyone's potential, nor take somebody for granted; and it supported the case for always treating people as individuals, whoever they might be.

I was aware that she already belonged to a close knit family but at some stage on her personal journey they must have been particularly proud of what she had achieved.

Hercules

I was asked to test the (Defence) Early Warning System one morning at the police station where I worked. I was required to switch on the system at a given time, listen to the spoken code word, write it down on a card and place it into the despatch box for return to the District Civil Defence Headquarters.

At 8 am I did what I had to do and listened to the code word, which was 'Hercules'. After dealing with the card and placing it securely in the despatch box, I telephoned my wife to say that I was on my way home for breakfast.

"Hello," I said, "Hello Hercules," she replied. "Why did you say that?" I gasped. She said, "I don't know, I just did." I said, "But you have never said that before, and that's our code word for the day, which no-one is supposed to know!"

The answer to his prayers

I happened to have been on duty when a minister of religion was arrested and brought to the police station. He had been seen by other drivers weaving his car from one side of a main road to the other, due to being well under the influence of drink.

I particularly liked this person for the remorse he showed and he made profuse apologies to me before explaining that he had drunk too much after being involved in a domestic problem at home, which he very much regretted. He had a very Welsh name and he also lived in Wales.

I apologised whilst explaining that he would have to sleep in a cell overnight, until he blew a negative breath test before he could be released to make his way home in the morning. After assessing him as no risk to anyone's safety, I gave him an extra mattress and left his cell door slightly ajar.

In the morning I released him pending analysis of his specimen of blood and I wished him good luck.

A week later I saw the officer who had arrested him and asked about the result of the blood analysis. He told me he had just heard that the scientific officers had accidentally spilt the specimen and it could not therefore be analysed.

As the incidence of drunken driving was unlikely to be repeated, because he seemed to have genuinely regretted this lapse, I was actually rather pleased.

The following day, I received a radio message for me to return to meet someone at the police station and I found that the very same minister of religion had called by to see me. He thanked me for the considerate way in which he felt I had dealt with him after he had been arrested and he presented me with a small book about the bible, for which I, of course, thanked him most sincerely.

He said to me, "I very much regret my behaviour, and I have been praying ever since and my parishioners have been praying for me too."

After having purposely kept my body language in check for a while, I then somewhat gleefully told him, "You will be very pleased to know that your prayers have been duly answered, for there will be no further action against you, at all!"

The minister was very amused to hear what had happened to his specimen of blood!

An idyllic hamlet - a gruesome incident

It never failed to amaze me that, whilst the English countryside was so idyllic, so much violence erupted even there from time-to-time.

You would never imagine that in places with such fairy tale names as Dingle Dell, you were likely to be called to arrest someone who had just planted an iron bill-hook into the head of a neighbour.

Shortly afterwards, yet another bad tempered resident had swung a lump hammer into the face of his so-called friend.

Some people just feel compelled to express their anger and disturb the most tranquil of pastoral settings by flexing their muscles and creating havoc in one form or another.

Gone to bed - in their Wellies

When I called at a house with a colleague to speak to the person believed to be responsible for using the hammer, his landlady with a look of complete and utter innocence assured me that he had been in bed at the time of the assault!

Brian Breacher

When I insisted on actually speaking to him, I found him there in bed with his male accomplice – both fully clothed and wearing Wellington boots!

The one suspect readily admitted using the hammer to break the victim's nose and cheek and he was arrested.

Chapter 10: It Had to Be Experienced to Be Believed

A crossbow bolt through the head

My son once told me that his law tutor at University delighted in denigrating the police whenever they were the subject of discussion. I told him that it could well be that his tutor had not got a clue, for I sincerely felt that you had to be in this job to believe it, and to appreciate and understand it! I invited my son to spend the night with me when I was next on duty, so that he could see for himself. I gave him the freedom to spend his time wherever he pleased, and the next day he wrote an astute and comprehensive essay of his observations.

What immediately struck him at first, he said, was the completely calm and unflustered acceptance of a message that had been received from the local hospital.

It was brought to me for 'actioning', whilst I was briefing a team of officers before they commenced their various duties. The note was about a man who had been admitted to hospital with a cross-bow bolt through his head.

Gruesome or spectacular events of one kind or another were par for the course and were liable to occur on a daily basis.

Incidents such as this, accompanied by the associated action and a vast array of technical, physical and psychological challenges, confronted you almost every day. And they were not ordinarily within the common experience.

My son also took the view that my colleagues were very altruistic, though he thought they were inclined to be more tolerant of people's questionable behaviour than he regarded as generally fitting or deserved.

The police have no opportunity to refer to technical books when out in the street dealing with complex and fraught incidents; nor do they always enjoy support when it is needed most. They do not have the privilege of relaxing in the knowledge that their daily work will be neatly scheduled for them weeks in advance, rather like a Course Programme.

Improving my stamina

I dealt with just three men with particular religious backgrounds, whose negative assumptions and prejudices towards me as a policeman were so troubling that they made my stomach turn. Thankfully, the kind of darkness this created always passed after a fairly short period of time.

Their attitudes were so much out of sync with my usual experiences and they knew nothing about me as an individual. I had no idea where and how their people related perspectives had been formed.

Unfortunately my respect for them faltered a little as I came to regard their opinions and views with less enthusiasm than hitherto.

On each occasion after returning home following those encounters, I went for an eighteen mile run in the most peaceful of countryside, which I always thoroughly enjoyed.

I needed this form of antidote to help shrug off the possible effects of these occasional happenings, and sometimes for dealing with the lesser problem of confronting thugs. It gave me 'thinking time' to help clear my head of other people's baggage, so that I could begin the next day feeling completely refreshed. And it helped to restore a sense of rhythm and well-being into my existence.

Throughout the entire period of my service in the Police, I frequently went for five mile runs, but I embarked on the eighteen mile jaunts both during the day and at night-time every couple of weeks; or after meeting a particularly troubled individual or situation.

Of course, the church leaders whom I more usually had the pleasure of meeting, were generally inspiring, supportive, and responsible for initiating some brilliantly thought-provoking reflection. In any event, throughout my life I have always been a member of one church or another.

Keeping positive

Thankfully, being in the police service can produce a hugely rewarding feel-good factor from all the people who know you well; and from many others who appreciate what you do, or for whom you have given particularly satisfactory service.

It was important to have a range of relaxing, interesting and challenging leisure-time activities, entirely of your own choosing, to help maintain a positive outlook and offset the effects of working within a disciplined environment among people with disturbed lives and questionable attitudes.

I always benefited from a happy and active home environment and an immediate community of special friends. I felt that the love and respect of my wife was something to be earned, for her encouraging influence was always in the background, like the gentle flutter of an angel's wings.

Kicked in the head

Driving around a small town on my own early one afternoon, I happened to come across two eighteen year old youths. They were staggering along the pavement and frequently falling into the road; they were also very aggressive and abusive and very drunk. And as you have to start intervening in these affairs with an open mind, I asked them, "Are you two lads okay?" As well as becoming more abusive, they were obvious liabilities to themselves and a potential nuisance or threat to others.

I called for assistance to bring them to the safety of the police station and two colleagues arrived within just a few minutes. I handed one youth to them to take away, whilst I placed the other in the back of my car where he lay flat out on the seat, before I drove away.

I was travelling along the busy road towards the police station and as I steered into a fairly sharp bend I felt a kick in the back of my head from the individual on the rear seat, who was wearing boots.

As I drove out of the bend, I quickly slammed on my brakes to throw him off balance. I jumped around, knelt on my seat and firmly restrained the youth, so that I might continue my journey in safety.

I then looked up through the rear window, to see that a coach full of pensioners had stopped right behind me, within only three to four yards. Quite a few were gathered at the front of the coach, staring right into my car – with their mouths wide open! Within a very short space of time, their driver came hurrying to my door and said, "I just wanted to make sure you were okay but I can see you don't need any help!"

He had been very alert and public spirited, I thought, so I thanked him and with a very broad smile he returned to his coach. Both youths were taken to the cells to sleep until they were sober.

Brian Breacher

Sincerity

I once was asked to deal with an incident that might seem to have been quite unspectacular but which actually gave me an enormous amount of satisfaction. This was principally because it helped a young person with lots of potential to dig himself out of a real mess.

It involved responding to a request from a Grammar School Head Teacher, who was a well-respected professional and seemed to know something about every one of his pupils. He was always cooperative and very helpful whenever I went to see him 'on business' but at other times he could be extremely aloof.

He asked if I would deal with a young man aged fourteen years of age who in a moment of madness was suspected of stealing an expensive coat from a fellow student.

The head teacher told me that because he and his deputy both felt that this lad was responsible for the theft, they had altogether spent several hours interviewing him at school. They had become thoroughly exasperated with him and regarded the youth as extremely difficult after failing to persuade him to admit his indiscretion, or to recover the coat. I had no idea how they had attempted to deal with this task.

I took a young colleague with me to speak to the fourteen year old student in the presence of the deputy head teacher.

Depending on the kind of individual I would be confronting, I reckoned that my approach would probably need to be kindly, helpful and on his side, but firm and clear in my reasoning, and self-assured without being over-bearing.

You do not actually think through your approach before seeing the person involved but it flashes across your mind instinctively as soon as you meet, according to who and what you find before you.

I decided that my first task was to bring the young man back into the real world by securing his confidence in my ability to present him with a well reasoned argument. Then, mainly through my tone of voice, I needed to convince him that I sincerely had his interests at heart.

At the same time, I suggested that he now put aside the almighty mess he had so far made of this very difficult situation. I explained with empathy, that choosing to tell lies when in this kind of personal fix was a common phenomenon, with which I was very familiar. But his ill conceived, though understandable, reaction could still be overlooked. This, however, would be conditional upon his response from here on being far more clearly thought through.

Lastly, my responsibility was to lead him firmly towards making a bold and courageous decision, by persuading him to apply a little more wisdom than he had so far managed to achieve. I left him with the thought that the choice he was being asked to make was mighty important, requiring great forethought and maturity. An expression of intent was his alone to make and only he would receive any credit for deciding to tell the truth.

Including my preamble, it took twelve minutes for the lad to confess his guilt and to say where he had hidden the coat. The deputy head teacher stood there open mouthed with disbelief, as I left my colleague to take a written statement of the young lad's confession. The deputy head later exclaimed that he was amazed by what had been achieved with such a gentle approach.

I sincerely believe that the young lad was really pleased to have received some help in dealing with this problem for, had he not dealt with it satisfactorily, the reverberations would have been very serious for him indeed, well into the future!

A lack of musical appreciation

I was called to a public house at the edge of an area of beautifully unspoiled common land, where a middle-aged guest pianist had been entertaining the locals in a really pleasant and relaxed family atmosphere.

A gang of surly men arrived at the pub, but were turned away because of their intimidating presence.

After finding themselves outside, they decided to cause mayhem for the licensee. So they approached a front sash window close to where the pianist was performing and unceremoniously dragged the musician through the opened lower half of the window! Then they beat him up very badly before driving off into the night across the secluded common!

One of the customers managed to note down the number of their truck and passed this on to me. I took about eight officers with me and within twenty minutes we found the truck parked on an enclosed site about a mile away where a dozen or so people lived and worked temporarily. Our experienced dog handler was with us and he always carried a well gnarled seasoned stick with a solid knob on the end. He was accompanied by his handsome, disciplined and courageous German shepherd dog.

We stood in the middle of the compound asking questions of a couple of the inhabitants, when I noticed one of the resident dogs. A large black, battle scarred and ferocious beast had emerged from the darkened edge of the compound and was making its way cautiously and stealthily towards our dog handler. Its shoulders were hunched as it lowered itself then bared its teeth, before drawing menacingly closer!

The dog handler remained thoroughly calm as the savage dog came within about two feet of his Alsatian. Then, he raised his stick and very firmly brought the knob down squarely upon the dog's nose. It turned tail in an instant and raced off back into the undergrowth, never to threaten us again. The gang of assailants was duly processed and taken to Court.

Caravans on the common

I once humoured myself doing virtually nothing for a few days on the same idyllic common, where lots of complaints had justifiably been made about people illegally camped in their caravans in huge numbers making an almighty mess of this distinctly tranquil place.

I had been asked to spend a couple of weeks restoring the area to the usually pleasant condition that everyone enjoyed.

This was a very popular, natural environment, with many woodpeckers and nightingales and an abundance of other wildlife too. It was also an ideal location for walking or running and was regularly frequented by families with young children, who had now begun to stay away because of a perceived atmosphere of intimidation.

I decided to arm myself with a clipboard, pen and paper and spent about an hour in the morning and again in the afternoon, over a period of three days, walking around the site saying "hello" and "hi" to as many people as I could. I did very little else apart from exchange a few other pleasantries. I paused for a few moments here and there, which may have given the impression to the temporary 'residents' that I was taking an unhealthy interest in their vehicles, and perhaps recording a few details.

The aim was that everyone on site would feel obliged to match their manner with mine, so that no hostility would be shown towards me at any time; but there were quite a few quizzical glances!

Within just three days the whole Common was cleared without a cross word or any legal pressure whatsoever having to be applied.

Chapter 11: People Struggling to Deal With Pressure and Stress

Eleven holes punched through the walls

One evening a distraught wife visited the police station to tell me that her husband had gone berserk shortly after arriving home. She said she had only just managed to escape after seeing him punch eleven holes right through the interior walls of their home, before smashing their bath to pieces.

I went into his home, whilst my colleagues waited around outside. I approached him very gently, but confidently, and asked whether it would help him to share his problem with me. He explained that for the third time he had failed to pass his driving test! His wife had warned me that he could suddenly become volatile for what seemed to her to be quite inconsequential reasons.

I spent about an hour with the man sincerely and firmly persuading him that he ought, for his own sake and that of his wife, to be examined at the police station by two qualified specialists who I guaranteed would have his best interests at heart. A police station was then, and probably still is, classified as 'a place of safety' for this purpose.

A short while later, after he came with me to the police station, the process of persuading two psychiatrists to place him within the safety of a secure and caring environment for assessment, continued for two more hours.

They seemed very reluctant to commit him to a suitable hospital, but from my own perspective and having seen the condition of his wife and the damage inflicted to his house, he seemed desperately in need of secure, medical supervision on a temporary basis, at least.

Eventually and for a period of just seventy two hours he was taken into care for his own well-being and the safety of his wife. This brief respite helped him to get things in perspective.

The depressed physicist

The GP from a neighbouring village called at our police office one afternoon. He was extremely concerned for a patient, a metallurgist, who had jumped out of a window as the doctor arrived to examine him in his home.

He was really anxious for his patient's mental well-being and for any harm that could befall him or others whilst he was at liberty in such an unbalanced state.

He gave me his patient's description: thirty four years old, well over six feet tall and of athletic build, and I went to the village to find him. Within a very short time, I saw him walking aimlessly along the edge of the busy pavement looking a very agitated, confused and distressed figure.

I pulled up alongside him in my car and opened the front passenger door, asking him if he was okay. In response to his cry of "Fascist," I slowly drove forward and stopped the car at his side again. I asked if he would like to take a rest in the car and he climbed in.

After being seated for only ten seconds or so, he suddenly darted out of the car and prostrated himself face down on the road in front of oncoming traffic which, to their credit, just managed to stop in time!

I have to say that trying to persuade a six foot man into the back seat of a two door car with me keeping him company was no mean feat. Then, because I was without any means of communication, it was also less than straightforward persuading a somewhat bemused ambulance driver to drive the police car to the police station some six miles away.

Two psychiatric specialists were initially reluctant to assess someone they perceived to be a well-respected member of the community as mentally unstable, thereby committing him for a short period to the care of a hospital for assessment.

In every case, without exception, I was always puzzled by how long it took to convince these professionals of the potential risk mentally unstable patients were to their own well-being, let alone that of the public.

This was especially so when the psychiatrists were thinking of discharging an individual whilst he was in a clearly confused and disturbed condition, leaving him to wander the streets alone, at night-time and in the rain.

I did wonder whether, if they saw at first hand the outcome of the behaviour of severely disturbed people, they may have a greater understanding of police and public concerns. Failing to err on the side of caution, and deciding to release a patient who is in a state of depression, increases the likelihood of a mentally disturbed person injuring another or taking his own life.

When the police are left to formally release a patient because there is no longer a power of detention, and the person is alone without a suitable friend or family member, and still appears confused and distressed, they invariably feel that an inappropriate decision has been made. This always leaves them anxious or uncomfortable and concerned for everyone involved.

Chapter 12: Dealing With Extremes

The aggressive poacher

I received a complaint by telephone in the early hours of the morning from a very frightened gamekeeper. He told me he had just been intimidated by three poachers, one of whom had fired a shotgun, after the gamekeeper had gone outside his house to investigate a noise.

I was very familiar with the poaching laws as a result of managing several cases, so I was sufficiently confident when I arrived at the scene.

The gamekeeper described to me an encounter he'd just had with an aggressive poacher from a nearby town, who he knew well because he had more than once been threatened by him during previous confrontations.

I took a statement from him and he warned me to be on my guard when visiting the poacher with the gun. I then went with my colleagues to the suspect's home at 2.20 in the morning and knocked hard on his door.

The officers accompanying me warned me of his propensity for violence which was well known to them. I told them that I would go into the house on my own, for I wanted him to fully take in what I was going to say without in any way being distracted.

When he opened the door I stepped inside and told him that I was arresting him for discharging a loaded firearm with intent to endanger life, which is unmistakably a very serious crime. The worst he had expected was to have been accused of poaching which he would then have immediately denied. However, the result was that he was completely taken aback by what I had said and he offered no resistance whatsoever.

He was taken to the police station looking extremely anxious and was placed in a cell where, I was reliably informed, he worried all night about the dire implications of what he had been accused of doing.

In the morning when I spoke with him, he earnestly assured me that he had only been poaching, which I then readily agreed to accept. He pleaded guilty in Court and never bothered the gamekeeper, nor did he attempt to intimidate him, ever again!

Recognising insincerity

When dealing with all manner of people, you need the ability to assess the evidence, recognise truth from fiction and, at the same time, to be aware of any underlying psychosomatic issues, if possible. This is altogether an interesting challenge that keeps you on your toes.

It calls for a determination to deal effectively with those seeking to exploit the system for their own ends, alongside an interest in identifying and supporting the more vulnerable, if you can.

I remember listening to an attractive blonde woman, who had been arrested by an experienced store detective for shoplifting goods of fairly high value at a local store.

She went to great lengths to protest her innocence and challenged us to say that she actually looked like a thief! She said she happened to be under considerable stress due to looking after her children in the crowded shopping centre.

She insisted she was not the kind of person who would steal and claimed that the amount of money in her purse showed there was simply no need for her to be dishonest. She was animated and indignant throughout and she appeared to be very emotional in her determination to display an attitude of innocence.

She worked very hard to try and validate what she claimed was the store detective's mistake.

Just then another officer happened to come into the room. He enquired as to the reason why the woman was being interviewed. He then told me that he recalled seeing her going to a car a couple of hours earlier with her arms full of clothes.

Her car keys were found in her possession and two officers were sent to the car, where they recovered several hundred pounds worth of stolen items. When presented with the additional evidence of dishonesty, the woman became less vocal but shrugged her shoulders and smiled as if to say "Well, you can't blame me for trying!"

People of this woman's ilk are very much deserving of blame, for they force the authorities to always keep doubt in mind, even on those occasions when there might be a genuine need for a far more sympathetic approach.

Experience can be helpful

On another occasion I recall being in an adjoining room to where a middle-aged woman was being interviewed for shoplifting. I pricked up my ears when I happened to sense that something was amiss that the interviewing young officer seemed not to have noticed. I asked whether I could spend a few moments with the lady.

She was an elegant woman who happened to be the wife of a local professional person. She displayed a mixture of remorse, embarrassment and confusion and had great difficulty in accounting for her behaviour, for she seemed to be quite distracted.

I asked whether there were any ongoing personal problems in her life that she could explain to me. She told me there were difficulties with her marriage and that her teenage son had just been diagnosed with cancer.

I advised her as to how the current allegation could best be dealt with so that she would avoid proceedings. This helped place her more at ease in so far as this particular episode of her life was concerned.

The perverse use of charm

At another time, I was obliged to caution a well-known entertainer who had essentially used his charm to steal a trolley-load of foodstuff from a local supermarket.

Upon entering the shop he had feigned confusion and naivety to an assistant, and asked her to help him with his shopping. He continued to charm the lady throughout his sojourn with her around the aisles.

But she remained alert and did not allow herself to become beguiled or distracted. After he walked with the fully laden trolley straight past the tills and out into the street, she promptly arrested him and he was brought to the police station.

He continued to use his charm there, as I began to explain what was going to happen and why. I accepted some of his sweet-talking, but turned to a more firm and realistic approach after he sought to intimidate me by saying that the commander of the police division was a very 'close friend' of his.

I had to bring him back down to earth by gently telling him that apart from the bare-faced fact of his stealing, his method of causing extreme embarrassment to the store assistant was unlikely to be an image or quality that he would want made known to a clear-thinking public.

I really didn't know why he had begun to do this sort of thing but I was told that it was not the first time he had been suspected of shoplifting, by any means. An appropriate examination may well have explained his disposition.

Dealing with someone in authority

When handling people who attempt to use a position of authority to distract you from your enquiries, the adrenalin rush you experience can make the restoration of honesty and coherence into the equation even more satisfying than usual.

The collection of evidence in such cases may need to be very astute and detailed and the weak spots have to be exploited even more energetically.

When the suspect also uses emotional blackmail to persuade a friend to tell lies on his behalf, there is a huge range of counter-arguments that can be brought to bear, which can be extremely persuasive, especially when the risk of conspiracy and imprisonment is laid bare.

Chapter 13: The Attendance Centre

Later on when I was forty and for the last twelve years of my service, I moved to a much larger town where, in my spare time, I became manager of an Attendance Centre.

This Centre was set up at a school in this instance, though it was not at all run like a school. It was sponsored by the Home Office, for the benefit of young men aged 10 to 17 years who had become involved in crime and were required by the Courts to spend time there on Saturday afternoons, under my supervision.

The idea was to provide a disciplined, but caring, hard-working and purposeful environment, where time would be spent partly engaged in energetic physical activity and partly occupied in creative, craft-based tasks – which seemed to work very well.

I chose to run craft activities of wood-turning, acrylic work and wrought-ironwork, and had a staff of three teachers and an engineer. The number of lads attending averaged twenty-four, and they spent a period of two hours there every other week.

To set the scene, I kept the level of discipline firm, but during the craft sessions there was always emphasis on more imaginative activity, which then created different opportunities for making a more productive connection with these lads.

One of the teachers once told me that this "little blighter" who was in his wood-turning workshop had made a beautiful wooden vase on the lathe, but whilst in his class at school during the week, he never made anything!

I needed to keep the discipline at a high level, for if the lads suspected I was a soft touch, they would risk missing a session or two, which would then mean I should return them to Court. There was a constant requirement to deter them from appearing again before the magistrates to face a more severe sentence, but they were probably unaware of the dynamics of this common-sense reasoning.

They did, however, react well to firm and clear direction and were always noticeably pleased and satisfied with what they managed to achieve at the Centre, which was almost always quite impressive.

A probation officer once told me that some of these lads had recently been in his waiting room talking about the Attendance Centre and happened to remark that I was 'a reasonable bastard'. I thought I could live with that image for, coming from them, the probation officer and I regarded it as quite a compliment; at least I sincerely hoped it was. Hiccups sometimes still occurred but generally they could be resolved without too much difficulty.

The head-teacher of the school where the Centre was held, took the physical training classes. He once brought a seventeen year old lad to me because of his indiscipline. The lad confronted me in a defiant and aggressive attitude, as if to challenge my authority. I bawled at him with my nose about an inch away from his, which seemed to subdue him sufficiently for the time being.

But I needed then to quickly restore his confidence and trust in me for the right reasons, so I talked softly and asked if he loved his mum. He immediately began to relax and told me that he did. I asked the same of his dad but his response was different, for clearly he was very unhappy about the way his dad behaved towards him and his mother.

I invited him into my office to sit down in a calm environment with me and to talk about this problem, which we did at length.

I endeavoured to show as much genuine respect for him as I could, for his feelings and his point of view regarding his situation at home.

We parted on really positive terms and he was never a problem again. It can be very productive and satisfying if you manage to convince young people that without exception you always have their interests at heart.

The problem was that he was very self-conscious about the limitations of his personal hygiene, due mainly to having only one set of clothes to wear. I told him that I could not make any firm promises but I would see what I could do for him.

Back at the police station I telephoned several charities until I managed to connect with someone in London who seemed to speak the same language. He immediately understood when I said that I was trying to help this seventeen year old lad to hang on to his dignity.

The police force could be a very useful and persuasive base for enlisting support towards genuine need. Within a week – on Good Friday in 1982, I received a cheque for £100 from the London based charity, which was extremely generous at that time.

I then visited the local M & S store and introduced myself to the Store Manager. I told him of this lad's plight and asked if he could help stretch this money a little further. Quite amazingly he unhesitatingly gave me a voucher for £20.

I telephoned the lad and we went shopping at the same store for a full set of clothes. As he tried them on, the broad grin on his face was quite a sight to see. I cut off all the labels afterwards so that his family could not return them to the store for a refund. We then wrote a 'thank you' letter to the Charity.

A year or so later, I happened to meet this same youth again near a corner shop where I lived. He came over to me and we shook hands and had a chat together. I was thrilled that he seemed a great deal happier at that time.

I always looked forward to being at the Attendance Centre, which I managed for ten years altogether until I retired.

My last day of service

In my final day of service when I was leaving this vocation, through a brief speech I made, I thanked the criminals for their relentless challenge! I expressed appreciation to my colleagues for their generosity and I acknowledged my doctor's support for the occasional dose of Valium – *only joking!*

The incidents I have mentioned were just a small part of my overall police adventures; and involvement in this service had been an amazing experience that very few people could fully understand; all my initial expectations had been exceeded!

The chief constable asked to see me a week or so after I had retired from the police service; and in his office he produced my personal file and told me that I would find the contents "very interesting!"

I said, "Yes, I am sure I would." I then told him of the negative feelings I had experienced when I first joined the service and in particular of two young colleagues who I was expected to look up to as exemplary role models but who I did not view as 'real people'.

In the course of time, they both got themselves into serious trouble. And although I might have been green from the valleys of Wales at the time, I felt that I had been more perceptive than the individual of rank who was in charge of an early significant course that I was attending, who clearly thought the sun shone from them.

I pointed out that I had not joined the police to look for role models, for I had plenty of those in the robust and supportive coal-mining community from where I came.

The trust I had in my own instinctive feelings, relative to my own values, beliefs and experiences, had always stood me in good stead throughout my service so far as I was concerned.

I believe that the Chief Constable understood exactly what I was saying, for he told me that he had never felt more respect for anyone who had sat in the chair before me. At his request I then endorsed and signed his record book: "Thanks for everything", which I really meant. He said to me, "And thank you too."

I then drove home with just a small tear in my eye, and a feeling that a worthwhile career was finally complete.

I had a great deal of respect for many of my colleagues who I was very proud to work alongside. They demonstrated resilience, courage and selflessness in all manner of situations. They were extremely committed and in particular their wit and sense of humour could be incredible.

Within a few days, I received letters from the Magistrates in two different areas and from the head of the District Probation Service for my personal contribution towards the criminal justice system. I was particularly appreciative of their comments.

Chapter 14: The Young People's Befriending Scheme

By the time I retired from the police service, I was well aware that many of the young people I had met had every reason to feel disillusioned with their lives. Countless numbers were without decent leadership at home and they had little or no opportunity to influence what went on around them.

I set up a registered charity so that young people aged 10 to 17 years could receive a 'mentor' or 'befriender' if they were struggling to cope with a range of personal or home-based problems. I did this with the help of a hard-working secretary, a very supportive management committee, and many superb volunteer befrienders from all walks of life, including a few with past criminal convictions, who were equally successful.

I was never short of suitable volunteers, for there is a vast resource of talented, willing and amazing people out there, in every community.

The charity ran for fourteen years with a success rate of between 82 – 92% throughout the period of its entire existence, for young people who wanted to make this happen.

This meant that there was evidence they had moved their lives forward with significantly improved confidence.

Referrals were made to the project by the local Child and Adolescent Psychiatric Department of the General Hospital, the Children's Services, the Children's Society, Schools, individual parents, and others.

My initial task was to write an administration and training manual and apply for funding; then to recruit, interview, train and select the volunteers, who were mostly female.

I interviewed each young person with a view to matching them with a suitable volunteer, appropriate to their particular needs, on a one-to-one basis.

I provided the guidelines as to what should happen when they first met and for each subsequent two hourly session, initially for a total period of six months. But the bond often became so strong that they continued seeing each other of their own choosing, for three to four years or more.

The idea was to make a suitable match, so that each unhappy young person was provided with a window into a different kind of world.

To give them someone who would listen to them properly and to whom they could speak in confidence about any anxieties, problems, concerns or aspirations. Then to look forward to seeing each other every week; as well as engaging in purposeful activities together at every meeting.

After this scheme had run for a year or so, I came home one day and realised that all of these young people had a total of ten to eighteen problems out of about twenty-three or more recognisable categories, which made them extremely vulnerable.

I set about identifying and writing them down, and from that time onwards I used this list, which proved to be a useful guide to assess the justification for taking each young person onto the Scheme.

There is no doubt that excessive problems of this kind can be really dispiriting for young people.

Multiple home-based problems, included:

Addiction – to drugs, alcohol or nicotine.

Poor school attendance

Single parent – pre-occupied with work, partners, etc.

Relationship problems – with parent's partners, etc.

Peer pressure – at school or in the neighbourhood.

Financial problems – creating an anxious household.

Parent deceased – causing major problems.

Constantly 'put down' – even unwittingly by parents.

Lacking guidance – which can be frustrating for children.

Bullying outside of the home – and struggling to cope.

Seeing the child psychologist – for a variety of reasons.

Special educational needs – and associated problems.

Anger control issues – needing careful management.

Separation of parents in progress – bringing considerable problems.

Physically or sexually abused – needing astute handling.

Absent father – most fell into this category.

Low self-esteem – not surprisingly.

Parents with ill-health – creating a difficult environment.

Family member involved in crime – placing the whole family at risk.

Uninspiring home environment – which can be embarrassing.

Witnessing violence in the home – perpetuating an attitude.

No role model – desperately in need of a suitable mentor.

Parents unable to cope – and in need of assistance.

This project was very much a story about love in action, so are you sitting comfortably?

How did these problems manifest themselves?

a. I visited a sixteen year old lad who lived with his single father and whose mother had left him when he was a baby. His father really struggled to cope and there were signs that he was probably a bully and a racist.

The lad had acne, a squint, a slight speech impediment and special educational needs. I thought briefly about who could manage him and feel comfortable in his company, but the answer was very obvious. I matched him with a black woman who was a very strong-willed and caring school matron.

I knew she could not only handle the dad but become a role model for him too and show him the best way forward, for she possessed all the inherent and professional qualities necessary for this task.

Soon after I introduced her to the young lad, she arranged a special meeting at school for herself, the head-teacher and the special needs tutor, which proved to be very productive, for they set up a period of tuition to address his particular needs.

She took the lad to get some decent spectacles and visited the doctor to deal with his acne; her calming and caring influence even helped with his speech. She then organised a period of work experience for the youth, which he enjoyed.

His confidence and self-esteem began to blossom immediately and from their third meeting he started to call her 'Mum'.

b. I met a family where the fourteen year old son tended to sulk a lot and lacked confidence; he had been stealing from his mother's friends. He lived in a rather uninspiring home without a suitable role model. I spoke to the lad but he wouldn't look me in the eye and seemed unprepared to listen to what I had to say.

I tried a strategy that amazingly worked every time! I said to him, "Look, I'm not a double-glazing salesman you know. If you don't get your brain into gear and listen to what I have to say, you won't see my backside for dust. I'm not wasting my time here with you, you know!" I then went to the door and said I was leaving. A broad grin came over the lad's face and he apologised and asked me not to go.

I then took all the details I needed and whilst doing this I again thought about a suitable befriender for him. I told the mother that I had a woman in mind to be his befriender. But the mother asked if I could find him a man.

I said to her, "Well, not only is she a woman but she is black and she is so lovely that she absolutely glows." I asked the lad if he fancied that and he had no problem with such a positive image, at all.

I matched them together and he thrived so much from knowing her and being with her, that he made huge strides forward in a very short space of time. His befriender told me how trustworthy he was when in her home; she really enjoyed his company and he was delighted to be invited there for Sunday dinner, for a very long period of time.

c. Fifteen year old Malcolm's dad was a bus driver who agreed to Malcolm having a befriender after he had been caught stealing.

Malcolm rarely saw his mum who lived elsewhere, so I gave him a female mentor who was already in a very busy line of work with an International company.

She sometimes spent a little time at his home when picking-up Malcolm or setting him down afterwards, which enabled her to grasp a better understanding of his general circumstances. His father had a tendency to be tactlessly blunt about what he thought of his son, though his befriender had no doubt that they both loved each other a great deal.

He often complained that his son was dishonest for constantly raiding the fridge, as well as lazy and disrespectful.

"A case of learnt behaviour!" came to the befriender's mind one day, when she was in the garden admiring the well-finished extension that Malcolm's father had built.

"That must have been a long hard project?" she remarked to his dad. "Oh well, I've been off on long-term sick with a bad back, so I had plenty of time to do a proper job," he replied with total nonchalance.

She also noticed that his dad often interrupted when she was talking to Malcolm, telling him not to be "so stupid!" As well as that, he even boasted that he never bought oil for his car as he always managed to bring some home from work!

The befriender, through sheer dedication and energy, good humour, patience, understanding and commitment, turned this lad around and set him up with a completely different frame of mind.

She was a generous soul who gave the lad more than one opportunity to enjoy the experience of dining out in a restaurant, for this was something he had not previously experienced. His confidence grew to such an extent that instead of having to be persuaded over the doorstep, he enjoyed giving the order for the meals to the waitress himself.

He was also taken to see an open-air production of Shakespeare's Romeo and Juliet held in College grounds at Cambridge. Here his befriender had to use all kinds of body language to dissuade him from creating the rustle, rustle; crunch, crunch sounds, which were swiftly followed by "tut, tut" from the ladies sitting behind, as he dipped into a family size bag of crisps, during the silent scene of Juliet's death! He was so used to eating popcorn at the local cinema.

Yet to his credit, he managed to hold down a job and open a bank account far quicker than a youth of the same age, with a private and university education, who was too aloof to make his acquaintance when given the opportunity to do so on that same day.

d. I went to the home of a twelve year old boy whose parents had dumped him when he was little more than a baby. He had been in foster care for the past eight years far away from where his extended family lived. He was so unhappy that he was brought back to the area to stay with his grandparents. They and their home were uninspiring and they had no car and no spare cash, so he was seldom taken anywhere of interest.

When I spoke to him about having someone special all to himself, he fairly swooned at the idea. I matched him with a young but mature woman and when I introduced her to him, he simply couldn't wait to be with her on his own.

As they went off for their first couple of hours together, he gently asked if he could hold her hand, which of course he did. I wished I had been able to take a picture of them just then, for it would have encapsulated everything!

When I rang his grandmother the next morning to make my usual check on his initial reactions, she said, "He loves her to bits and can't wait for her to come again next Tuesday; apparently they are going to the Safari Park."

The befriender was still seeing this young man three years later, and he changed into a far happier and more confident young person.

e. My idea of a successful referral was sometimes at odds with other people's views. For example, a deputy head teacher once told me that a fifteen year old youth who she had referred, after about three months, still had a poor school record of attendance.

To her his story might have been a failure but to me it was an unmitigated success. Due to pressure of work, I imagine, the teacher had never visited the lad's home, so her knowledge of his background was apparently quite limited.

She was unaware of the entirety of his situation: that his father had died from taking drugs and his cousin was in jail for dealing in cannabis; he was very unhappy about a series of boyfriends his mother brought to their house; his home was quite uninspiring; and a neighbour had recently been arrested for interfering with his younger brother.

His befriender had only recently updated me by telling me that he had never once missed an appointment with her and they really enjoyed the time they spent together. She and I felt that he had actually made 'considerable' progress.

f. After visiting yet another fifteen year old youth, his mother came with me to the door when I promised that I would do my very best to find a suitable befriender for her son; they lived in extremely miserable circumstances.

She was in tears through being overwhelmed by the hope she had been given that their situation might improve; and I prayed that I could live up to her expectations.

I soon matched her son with a systems analyst who I knew very well and who had already earned my every confidence, due to previous successes.

When I rang the mother a few months later for an update, she assured me that the befriender was the best thing that had ever happened to them.

She told me he was reliable and professional and her son was always happy with whatever they did together; and he never let her son down, which was something they had never previously experienced in their lives!

g. Another fifteen year old lad was particularly saddened because his mother was suffering from cancer; and he had never known his father. After she died in the local Hospice, he remained with his step-father who was very caring and compassionate, but who struggled to cope on his own.

I matched the step-son with an extraordinary female befriender, who was incredibly capable, caring, perceptive and committed.

When she was first getting to know him, she told me that he had said to her, "If you asked me to explain how I feel about my life, it would be like inviting me to describe a colour that I had never, ever, seen before!"

h. Many young people regarded their parents as the primary source of their problems. One lad always came home from school to an empty house because his mother was so pre-occupied with work, socialising and boyfriends.

i. Another mother once told me that she just did not know why her daughter was so difficult. The parents (mother and step-father) were professional people and I had arrived at their home to see whether I could find a mentor for their fifteen year old daughter. Before I left, I asked to speak with the young lady in private for the last couple of minutes.

In confidence, I enquired as to whether she liked her step-father, and she told me that she did. I then asked if she got on well with her mother's current boy friend but she assured me that she did not.

"What about the previous one and the one before that?" I said. "I didn't like either of them," she replied. Where is your dad?" I queried. "He lives a long way off in Kent," she answered sadly. "Do you love your dad?" I asked. "Oh yes I do, but I don't see him often and I miss him a lot," she said.

"How do you cope with all of this?" I explored. "Well, this is what it's all about," she assured me. "My mother really does my head in!!" I found her a befriender who she saw regularly each week and who helped her to cope much better with all these personal issues.

j. Lastly, I took on a very lively twelve year old, whose befriender clearly found her task worthwhile, in a very exhausting sort of way. He lived with his mother who had been brought up in a children's home. She had several children and a new baby and another boyfriend; all-in-all she really did struggle to cope but she was an extremely likeable character.

Near Christmas-time for each of the past eight years, I had received a telephone call from a very special lady who wished to provide a Christmas parcel to a family less fortunate than her own.

She had rung me on this particular day for me to nominate someone to receive this year's gift. I always checked that the person I had in mind was comfortable about being recommended.

I was also running a training session for our befrienders the same evening, which I did through being an official tutor with Adult Continuing Education, a local organisation. At the same time, I always enjoyed providing some positive feedback to our volunteers.

I rang this young lad's mum and first asked if she was okay. She told me that she was having a very exhausting day due to a few domestic problems that were particularly tiresome. I asked if she would like a really nice Christmas parcel and she cheered-up immediately. She also told me how much her son was benefiting from being with his befriender who he thought was very, very special.

That evening at our training session, I was visited by an official observer for A.C.E., who sat in with the class for the whole of the period. I related a few success stories during the lesson, including the one about the lively young lad whose family I had chosen to receive a generous gift.

The following morning the observer rang me to say how much she had enjoyed the whole session. She also asked if she could donate her own (considerable) Christmas gift to yet another family whose needs I felt were equally deserving.

I chose a hard-working mother with a large family and adorable children whose husband had deserted her and whose boyfriend was in prison.

Many of the young people existed in such dark environments that to share any more of their stories might put them at risk of being identified and feeling uncomfortable.

In total, I took on nearly four hundred young people whilst running this project.

What made the Scheme work – the befrienders' qualities?

You may gather from what I have already said that the befrienders were indeed very, very special - and they certainly were. Over the years, I kept a running list of some of the qualities I identified in the successful befrienders, which made the scheme work so well.

Here are those worthy assets:

They each brought their own brand of personal magic.

They won the young people's trust and showed they cared.

They knew when to keep their distance – for young people don't like officials getting 'in their face'.

They provided a refreshing window into a different way of life.

They shared uplifting experiences.

They had great communication and listening skills.

They were relaxed, informal and flexible.

They had individual styles.

They were not overburdened with high case-loads.

They had the ability to connect.

They were not emotionally involved.

They showed unconditional, non-judgmental acceptance.

They were loyal and committed and never set them up to fail.

They were unpaid and involved in their leisure-time.

They had insight, patience and supportive energy.

There was thinking-time between sessions.

They were not hidebound by time or by too many rules.

They identified each young person's strengths and told them.

They helped them to solve their own problems and taught them how this could be achieved.

They identified trigger points.

They treated them like adults.

They encouraged them to make their own choices.

They helped to liberate them with self-belief and a clear idea of the kind of person they wanted to be.

They helped their confidence to grow from friendship and trust.

Most importantly, they did not excuse the young person's inappropriate behaviour, but taught them that everyone makes mistakes though we have to take responsibility for making them.

The more successful befrienders were unquestionably strong and not easily put off; nor surprised by the occasional set-back - for they knew that this was why the young people had been referred to us. They all had loving and caring, dynamic but modest personalities.

No charge was ever made to the referring agencies or to the families concerned. I received a £130,000.00 grant over six years from the National Lottery Fund, with the balance coming from the Local Council, a few other National Companies and local charities.

What I experienced, through seeing so many young people transformed from despair to hope, was near spiritual and it often made me tingle all over. I suspect that many of the young people and the befrienders themselves, as well perhaps as the odd parent too, experienced something similar.

It was not so much the Scheme itself that was responsible for this accomplishment but the interactive magic created by the personal chemistry generated between each pair that made sure these amazing relationships flourished.

Chapter 15: Afterwards – Filling the Gap

Adventure

After retiring and my wife's untimely death when she was just 48 years of age, I was determined to maintain a life-style that would include adventure and a flavour of freedom; as well as a chance to see how other communities lived; and to take on a far less serious, more relaxed role.

I began by visiting Istanbul and viewing the remarkable monuments there, the mosques and palaces, and the delicious food and market places.

I went trekking in the Himalayas for three weeks, which was an amazing adventure.

The welcome was warm and genuine and the ice capped mountains were breathtaking. The people lived in a very harsh though beautiful environment and worked extremely hard; and they all seemed so happy.

Then Syria - where on the first day during the journey from Damascus to Baniyas, I was held up for just a minute or so at gunpoint on a mountain road by six roughly dressed men, each carrying either a rifle or a machine-gun. But this was a fleeting experience and not an ordeal, and I was not robbed or in any way abused.

I walked the biblical mountains alone and was invited into house after house and given food and drink by the most hospitable of beautiful people.

They lived for each other in very caring communities, where hospitality and camaraderie seemed to be the most important components of a very special way-of-life.

When spending some time in Sicily, I might have shared a restaurant with a few Mafioso. I could have been mistaken, but they certainly projected that kind of stereotypical image and the nearest city happened to have the highest crime rate in Italy. I enjoyed many walks there and lots of decent restaurants too. I noticed that the more expensive houses were heavily guarded by dogs and elaborate electronic gates, which told a worrying story.

Then the U.S.A. – where people indulged themselves to excess, but there was unlimited opportunity for living and working in a free and democratic environment; and for adventure in the wide open, spectacular spaces. I visited the Rio Grande area, the Pecos and Apache Mountains, Wyoming, South Dakota and Yellowstone Park.

Next was Belize – to visit the people, the jungles, the crocodile rivers, Mayan temples, white sands and coral seas.

India came afterwards, where I and a friend stayed with the Mahdibagh Community of Bhora Muslims for five weeks during their annual wedding celebrations.

They were extraordinary people, very religious, confident, handsome, progressive, well educated and justifiably proud of their culture, and with ambitious, well-supported children.

But they lived in the midst of many extremely poor people, who, nevertheless seemed in most cases to be happy. Many of the Bhora Muslims were trained as doctors, scientists and business people, and were involved in making a difference all around the world.

Indonesia was next on my list, where I stayed with my daughter-in-law's family and friends on a very small island. People here were friendly and generous too, even though they were quite poor. Children were given beautiful names, such as Farah Noor (beautiful light) with meanings they would be proud to live up to.

The landscape was fertile and spectacular, and the people especially cared a great deal for each other. Unstinting support was available at all times, together with incredible personal warmth.

Many were also ambitious and determined to improve their way-of-life, but needed to go further-a-field to places such as the U.S.A. in order to progress. Many returned afterwards with their wealth, knowledge and qualifications, to help and share with the communities they loved most. I was particularly impressed by the friendship shown and how people relaxed and thrived when in each other's company.

I visited a brick mine in a cave on the island and was struck by the men and women who were happy together, even though they were busy hacking stone from the wall of a cave. Incredibly, there was a ninety year old woman settled on her haunches smashing up soft broken stones to make binding powder for the bricks.

Bali itself was a special experience and full of the most amazing wood carvers, with ample luxury for visitors to enjoy.

In the Pyrenees I spent a few periods of quiet reflection walking the hills where the vultures and eagles were in absolute abundance. People were friendly here too and the food was always plentiful and delicious.

Brian Breacher

All-in-all, I learnt a good deal about keeping an open mind, especially towards people who may at first sight appear different; and to view them as equals or as a healthy challenge, and often as a very welcome change rather than a threat.

I have seen individuals and small cliques everywhere, showing cynicism, ignorance and frighteningly irrepressible prejudice towards people they simply do not understand.

Quite possibly, a similar mentality has been at least partly responsible for giving birth to most of the world's dictatorships.

I spent a great deal of time amongst people who regarded themselves as ordinary, but whom I always viewed as special through them being indisputably genuine and sincere, warm, caring, modest, open, communicative, hard-working and astute, talented, humble; and each in their own way always endeavouring to make things better.

Or, put more succinctly, those more noble individuals in whose presence you always feel comfortable.

This awareness may have had something to do with why I became a member of the Bahá'í Faith – a fast growing religion that encourages a loving and forward thinking community.

This Faith originated in Persia in 1863 and values people whatever their religious beliefs, nationality, race or creed. They see the world as one people and one Faith with one God. But regardless of your beliefs or religious affiliation, if any, the manner in which you apply your own values, thoughts and energy on a daily basis is possibly what matters most of all.

It is a very special experience to be among those who put themselves out to produce the kind of chemistry that needs to flow freely so relationships may flourish – whatever their origins or beliefs.

Brian M Breacher – 3rd September 2008 ©